A Practical Guide to Ensemble Devising

A Practical Guide to Ensemble Devising

Davis Robinson

First published 2015 by
PALGRAVE

Palgrave in the UK is an imprint of Macmillan Publishers Limited, registered in England, company number 785998, of 4 Crinan Street, London N1 9XW.

Palgrave Macmillan in the US is a division of St Martin's Press LLC, 175 Fifth Avenue, New York, NY 10010.

Palgrave is a global imprint of the above companies and is represented throughout the world.

Palgrave® and Macmillan® are registered trademarks in the United States, the United Kingdom, Europe and other countries.

ISBN 978–1–137–46155–1

This book is printed on paper suitable for recycling and made from fully managed and sustained forest sources. Logging, pulping and manufacturing processes are expected to conform to the environmental regulations of the country of origin.

A catalogue record for this book is available from the British Library.

A catalog record for this book is available from the Library of Congress.

Printed in China

Contents

Figures

Acknowledgements

Thanks to all the actors, musicians, and designers of Beau Jest Moving Theatre, especially the founders – Elyse Garfinkel, David Russell, Karen Tarjan, Lisa Tucker, and Chris Wilder; to Larry, Steve, Lauren, Pat, Jay, Mimi, Phil, Judy, Robin, and Kathleen; and to my students and colleagues at Bowdoin College, Emerson College, and the Celebration Barn Theater. Special thanks to Lucy Knight, Jenni Burnell, and the reviewers at Palgrave for their help in editing this book; and to my life-long collaborator and most-honest outside eye, Libby Marcus, who steered Beau Jest out of many a pothole with insightful comments at the right moment.

Introduction

I was motivated to write this book after leading a weekend workshop on improvisation and devising for people who wanted to deepen their ensemble skills. Some participants had worked together in the past, some were new at it, but the point of the weekend was to spend time playing together in the studio from dawn to dusk. It was a magical weekend that left everyone feeling refreshed, revived, and ready to make new work. It struck me how easy it was to create those conditions, and yet how rare it was for people to take the time to do this kind of work together.

I think actors everywhere should have a chance to do what we did. Get up in the morning, move, and develop a common vocabulary, break for lunch, spend the afternoon problem solving and testing out ideas for material, eat dinner, go back into the studio for a night of improvisation and devising, showing and critiquing work which may get picked up the next day for further development or shelved forever. There was no effort to satisfy an audience besides us. No one was worried about whether the work will "sell" or entertain. It was just a chance to create disposable, interesting material. All of the participants have since gone on to work with other companies, and the freedom and skills they developed that weekend have paid for themselves many times over.

I find the process so satisfying, and so worth doing for the sheer pleasure of the doing itself that I am beginning to think that is the real value of ensemble theater making: the discovery of new ideas, the collective excitement of exploring the unknown. It is like meeting a group of friends outside an unexplored cavern and entering in together, moving from chamber to chamber of subterranean delights and fears. It is not, at first, a journey made for public performance. Developing a show for an audience happens later. The journey of discovery in the moment for actors is a valid end in itself. As more actors investigate this kind of work, and new ensembles are formed, the more difficult phase of creating performance pieces becomes a natural outgrowth of this initial phase of shared collective pleasure.

Ensembles develop a piece through trial and error, risk-taking, and experimenting. Mistakes become innovations that show up in the dramaturgy of the piece; creative struggles turn into dramatic, onstage relationships. Even when a linear story or an existing script is the start point for a piece, what distinguishes the ensemble approach is the degree of personal investment and experimentation that takes place in rehearsal, pushing the material to its limits and reimagining the piece through the collective vision of its artistic collaborators.

Ensembles rely on exploring the inherent theatricality of a moment. A spirit of physical trust, probity, and selflessness is needed. A script is often arrived at last rather than first. More than anything, ensembles are made up of people who are willing to try things without knowing or caring what the payoff will be for a while. This is a hard shift for some actors to make. It can be terribly frustrating when people disagree, but it is a necessary crucible for forging the best possible piece. In devising original work, objectivity, quality, perspective, interpersonal dynamics, and aesthetics are added to the usual rehearsal concerns of a company. It can sometimes feel like being lost in the woods, a feeling captured beautifully by Shakespeare when the Rude Mechanicals devised their version of Pyramus and Thisbe in *A Midsummer Night's Dream.* When Bottom takes charge of the play-making process and assigns all the best parts to himself, he drives his collaborators mad and makes an ass of himself. Their final show turns into a farce, not the high art they believed it to be. In writing this book, I hope to save you some time and agony while devising. But conflict is part of creativity, and despair inevitable. Do rest assured when you hit a low point: the problems you encounter as an ensemble have been faced by many others before you and are part of the process. There will always be strong wills and differences of opinion, and the Big Picture distance one needs to see their own work objectively is hard to find (Figure I.1).

The main focus of this book is on creating original material. For me, original material is where the real magic lies. Whether it's an in-class project cooked up in ten minutes by people who just met, or a professional company working all year on a major production, the challenges and rewards of ensemble creation are the same: it is the collective excitement and joy of theater making – exploring uncharted territories, creating a new image – the positive energy released when a group of artists create a moment of theatrical magic never seen before. When the stars are in alignment and the process works, the results are deeply satisfying for audience and performer alike. Even if an audience never sees the work, the process is

Figure I.1: *2008 Devising Workshop (Liz Pounsett and Megan Strell) at EepyBird Studios, Buckfield, Maine. Photo: Adam Montanaro*

invaluable for actors to experience. It satisfies a different part of the brain than the pleasure one gets from playing a role. It improves reflexes, and helps you reconnect with why you make theater in the first place.

Many colleges have added physical theater, devising, and ensemble work to their curriculum. People who are new to the process can find it immensely frustrating, especially devising something original with a group of peers and no leader. If a teacher or director tells a group to devise something with no leader assigned, everyone's strengths and weaknesses become apparent. There is no avoiding this crucible, and to some extent experiencing these negotiating difficulties is healthy. It is how we learn to navigate differences. This book helps actors, directors, and teachers learn to work constructively with each other. It prepares actors for the devised, adaptive, and innovative work that is increasingly appearing in the theatrical mainstream. It gives teachers and directors several models for guiding devised work. Early chapters tune up individual abilities that contribute to ensemble work. Later prompts give people ways to make material and stay on task. The last chapters cover the making of full-length shows with an ensemble.

Apologies if I misappropriate anyone's favorite exercise or describe it differently than the version you know. Please make this work your own. And apologies for my use of the term "you". Often I am talking to everyone "in the room". If you are a teacher, director, actor, or combination of all three, take the word in the way you most need it to apply. With devising, these roles are often merged. Usually I am speaking to "you" as the person leading an exercise or the person participating in it. This book is for students, teachers, and directors studying the devising process, and for existing ensembles looking for new approaches. My focus in the end is on professional companies making full-length work, but applications to the student deviser/director can be found throughout the book.

College programs will find the chapters on Fundamentals, Short Prompts, and Large Prompts useful, as these exercises can be done within typical academic time frames, in class or rehearsal. The latter half of the book focuses on professional theater companies and the complex task of creating full-length original and adaptive works. Colleges with programs focused on ensemble devising can do much of this work if enough time can be built into the academic schedule. My alma mater Hampshire College allows students to spend three years doing preparatory work for a year-long senior thesis, an academic model that works well for devising ensemble theater.

Commercially successful ensemble shows now appear regularly in mainstream theaters, and highly skilled dynamic ensemble performers are in short supply. The traditional ability of an actor to learn lines, play actions, and follow directions must expand in ensemble work to include stressful interpersonal demands, more dramaturgical questioning, and greater exploration of the boundaries of the material being worked on. The exercises and prompts in this book provide the training actors and directors need to join or start a devising ensemble, and guidelines for people interested in leading that work professionally or in an academic setting.

1 *What Is Ensemble Devising?*

Manifesto

Let's make a new world together. Let's go into a bright, empty, church-like space together, ripe for potential creation. A clean, roomy studio with good lighting, a few props and objects tucked into the corners, perhaps some fragments of history tacked to the walls or embedded in the architecture of the space revealing its origins as a mason's lodge, an Oddfellows Hall, a former factory, a church, a barn, an office, a garage. A window looking out onto a field or an ocean would be nice, but a view of 14th St. and 5th Ave. works just as well. In the back stairwell is an old poster of a group that performed here, a company that no longer exists, a press photo from some other time and place. Perhaps there's a pile of leftover office supplies from previous tenants that will end up in the piece you are making. I think many dance pieces are made using chairs because the main object found in every dance studio is a folding chair. If more rehearsal studios had chicken feathers sitting around, we'd probably see a lot more pieces involving wings, tickling, and flying. We use what we find, and what we bring to the table. And with ensemble theater, the primary ingredient is each other: our memories, our ideas, our desires, our fears.

How apt

We join together in secular communion to explore the wonder, mystery, joy, and pain of meeting each other and the world (Figure 1.1).

- What do I have to say? What can we, as a group, say?
- Who is that person?
- How does the world affect us?
- What is going on today?
- Can we create something that moves, laughs, provokes, and excites us?
- Can we dip a toe into the universal?

Figure 1.1: *Adam Klein, Dawson Hill, Amanda Houtari, and Stephen Volz, EepyBird Studios, Buckfield, Maine. Photo: Adam Montanaro*

The most fulfilling work often happens when you aren't under pressure to make something for public showing. In college classes and in workshops I've taught with professionals, the most inspired, wildly exciting material often happens in the studio where risks are freely taken and there is no need to edit or shape the material for an audience's expectations. You can run as fast and as far as the collective interests of the group will take you. There is no fear that you are committed to these people for life, or that your livelihood depends on having a commercial success. There is enormous value in this sheer act of shared collaborative creation for its own sake.
It recharges a performer's batteries, creates new friendships, gives insight into other points of view, and yes, valuable art gets made and thrown away every day, never to be seen by anyone other than the participants. But it's worth it. The monologue that was never written down, the perfectly executed physical image that captures the eye and disappears – these are the rewards of ensemble work in the moment (Figure 1.2).

Out of this practice, solid, professional work can grow. I encourage you to carve out a weekend, a week, or a couple of months to meet and do some of this work with friends and strangers with no goals in mind. Don't worry about writing a full-length piece, giving a name to your group, or producing a finished product. Just share exercises and make stuff up. Every time I make a new show with my theater company, Beau Jest, we allow plenty of up-front time for brainstorming and creative experiments. It is my favorite part of

Figure 1.2: King Lear, *Devising Intensive (Micah Williams and Steven Shema), Celebration Barn Theater, South Paris, Maine, 2013. Photo: Scott Vlaun*

rehearsal, and there is always a bit of a sense of loss when we have to shift gears and start locking things down to create the finished show. The work also gets a lot harder when you have to edit choices and polish every moment. Enjoy the early stages of work-for-work's-sake as long as you can, because the nuts and bolts of making a finished product will eventually take over and crowd out more liberated creative explorations.

So let's get started!

Speaking of which, a disclaimer. This book is not trying to present a comprehensive survey of all working methods used for devising. That would be impossible. The field is growing so quickly such a book would be out of date before it could be published. I am writing to share the methods I have encountered, and to provide guidance to students and artists interested in making the transition from mainstream theater to the world of ensemble devising. I work in Boston, Massachusetts, and Portland, Maine, so the groups and methods I am familiar with have a New England bias. I studied at Jacques Lecoq's school in Paris, France, and at the Celebration Barn Theater in South Paris, Maine, with Tony Montanaro, a mime who trained with Etienne Decroux and Marcel Marceau. Other influences include workshops with the dancer Mark Morris, Jonathan Wolken of Pilobolus, Ruth Malezcheck of Mabou Mines, Bill Irwin, Ronlin Foreman, and Keith Johnstone. I have seen some stunning shows in New York and Boston, but know that I have missed out on many exciting ensembles elsewhere. Devised work has a long history in England, and I have only caught glimpses of some of the seminal companies there. My apologies to the many fine people working in Minneapolis, Chicago, Atlanta, Austin, the West Coast, and elsewhere around the world who I haven't seen or mentioned. New groups are forming every day. It is a rapidly expanding field, and this book is in no way trying to keep track of them all or evaluate which ones are important.

This book is based on my own experiences as an actor, director, and teacher doing original ensemble work, and my desire to share the methodologies I've developed or encountered over time with others. I teach ensemble devising and physical theater at the college and professional level, and have for 30 years made work with a Boston-based theater company called Beau Jest Moving Theatre.[1] My most in-depth devising work is with Beau Jest, so I will reference that work often. I also reference other ensembles that make different styles of work to ensure the reader understands I am not endorsing any particular aesthetic here. When I teach devising, I work with open-ended exercises that allow the participants to develop their own aesthetic. What I include here are the exercises I return to most frequently as a teacher, director, and ensemble actor. I will try to notate whether an exercise I discuss is geared towards classroom work or professional companies. And I will also try to give you the lineage of an exercise when I know it.

Much has been written about internationally renowned ensembles such as Germany's Berliner Ensemble, Peter Brook's International Center for Theater Research, France's Theatre de Soleil, and seminal companies in America. Erwin Piscator's Dramatic Workshop, the Open Theater, and the Living Theater were all incubators of the ensemble spirit. Their omission here is in no way a comment on their importance to the field. Some of the productions I reference in this book were created by individual writers and directors, and not through ensemble devising, but I include them as dramaturgical models for the kind of work ensembles can aspire to. If you are interested in further research in the field, I have included an appendix with some of the main books discussing the history of ensemble theater, its origins, and the current state of the art. When I reference a show or ensemble, I will also provide the main web link to the company so you can follow up on their work.

Some definitions

When an ensemble decides to create an original show or radically restage a script, it enters into the world of "devising". For me, devising is the process of inventing material for performance together, including scene and script work, choreography, narrative structures, and design elements. The devising process applies equally to creating something original or adapting existing material and reframing it in a new way. The same skills are needed to develop a unified whole, whether starting from scratch or working from an existing source.

When problem-solving work is done collaboratively with everyone in the company in the same room – whether steered by a director, teacher, writer, or consensus – you are engaged in the process of *ensemble devising*. You can have an acting ensemble without entering into the devising process, and you can practice devising without having a permanent ensemble, but you can't devise a piece collaboratively with a group of people unless you agree on working towards a shared aesthetic. Some devising groups retain their artistic identity but change personnel from show to show (usually with a continuing core of artists making decisions). Other devising ensembles use a permanent repertory acting company with the same artists involved in every production, remaining true to their founding identity as a group while continuing to find new topics to explore.

Is there such a thing as ensemble work without devising? Yes, a good cast in any show can have a real spirit of ensemble by listening and working well together without inventing the show they are performing. In fact, many of the exercises in this book can be used in the rehearsal room to help traditional casts as well as devising ensembles become a more seamless group of players. Can a director lead an ensemble with little input from the actors? Of course: it happens all the time. A brilliant leader doesn't need input, they already know what kind of work they want to make. The company can function as a unified ensemble, and yet have very little input in the making of a show.

Ensembles can be as small as two people – a performer working with another actor, director, writer, or friend to create a solo or duet show – to a group as large as 20 or 30 people. My own company Beau Jest has fluctuated from shows with two characters to shows with 14. Of our original five founding members, most have been in at least five productions and two have been involved in all of them. When we began as a company, the term "devising" was not even in use. We simply called it making original work, or doing "physical theater", or movement-based, actor-generated work.

Can a person devise a show alone? Yes, but they usually have someone watch their work and help them, which I think also qualifies as devising. Can ensembles devise a great show with no one leading? I doubt it. My experience is that someone has to make decisions, great or not, so that you can move on. It is the endless arguing in early devising attempts that drives people mad. You must decide how your group will handle disagreements. This book explores how to work collaboratively on a project with the paradoxical knowledge that, at the same time, someone needs to steer the ship. Often this line is blurred. I don't endorse any one way of leading; that is up to you and your ensemble. Chapter 5 has suggestions for how to structure that hierarchy. It is likely that hierarchy already exists and you may just need help recognizing it.

A little history

While it appears that ensemble devising is a theater movement that started in the latter half of the 20th century, it really is part of a much older tradition already well established when Shakespeare captured the joy of the Rude Mechanicals meeting in the forest to devise a play for the Duke in *A Midsummer Night's Dream*. Peter Quince and company found ingenious, poor-theater solutions to portraying a wall, a moon, and a lion that wouldn't "fright the ladies", solutions that included meta-theatrical concepts truly postmodern in nature. And they had a great time doing it. Though played for humor in *Midsummer*, Shakespeare captured the spirit of ensemble creation, a form that welcomes all takers, all methods, and all themes. That same spirit pervaded the touring troupes of the Commedia Delle'arte in the 16th and 17th centuries, who barnstormed Europe with their spontaneous and inventive playing style. Before Commedia, the local merchant guilds and townspeople who formed ensembles to stage Mystery Plays in medieval times must surely have done some devising. And I am sure there were devisers in ancient Greece whose names we will never know who created shows full of theatrical innovation for the Festival of Dionysus, never written down and now lost to time.

The value of ensemble work

Working with an ensemble is a way of being in touch with the infinite. Watching a great ensemble perform, or *being* part of a group that spends time training together to become a fine-tuned organism, creating worlds triggered by memory, family, geography, nature, and images from the fantastic to the mundane, is a way of defining who we are as people and what we can do as artists. It's probably similar to the sense of excitement one gets playing on a successful sports team or has during a religious experience, or the pleasure one finds on a group camping trip, sitting around a fire at night laughing and telling stories. It's that effortless sense of one-ness, joy, and being totally alive, where time stops and we all breathe a collective breath. Ensemble theater allows us to experience humanity at its richest/deepest/sharpest.

In a workshop or educational setting, you can create an ensemble spirit in less than an hour. A day-long or week-long intensive workshop with a group of strangers learning a methodology together can lead to a sense within the group that it is a fully functioning ensemble that has worked together for years (albeit one guided by the instructor). It can also be a train wreck if there are combative personalities and conflicting aesthetic ideals. But when it works, people leave workshops or schools with new friends and collaborators who later become core members of future ensembles.

A laboratory atmosphere of experimentation is a core value of ensemble work. It is a form that keeps acting skills fresh and provides an outlet for creative impulses. It helps you learn as an artist what you have to say, and how best to say it. When you work as an ensemble to develop a piece, you put forth hundreds of ideas and offers that sink or swim over the course of creation. It is a training ground and forum for discovering which ideas are stageworthy. What line, image, thought, or moment works best? Does it end up in the final piece? This "cream rising to the top" effect is valuable for seeing which contributions last. It is humbling and empowering.

The ensemble production model

In the traditional process of putting on a show, producers choose a script, a director, a team of designers, and a cast of actors. The script is often by a famous playwright, now deceased. Everyone working on the show has a defined job. The company rehearses for three to four weeks, with pre-production work done ahead of time by designers and directors. In America, most of this work is done by non-profit regional theaters found in every state, or in the commercial theater industry centered in large cities like New York or Chicago. Most of the actors, directors, and designers are freelance artists who go from theater to theater looking for work. Playwrights submit their work for grants, festivals, and workshop opportunities. In a college setting, the faculty or department chooses the shows, assigns the design and technical work, and auditions the actors.

In the ensemble production model, artists band together and start their own theater company. This usually means a group meets and coalesces around some kind of shared artistic vision or goal. It could be to produce plays of forgotten playwrights, to recreate silent movies on stage, or to serve emerging voices. It could be to do work that serves a specific political or social mission, and it can happen at the college, amateur, or professional level. It may begin with the desire to serve a community that existing theaters/programs aren't reaching or to do work with a unique philosophy of performance. It may begin simply because people aren't getting enough work and want to give themselves a project to engage in. Actors may just want to create a show that challenges their acting, singing, and dancing skills. When all the artists involved help choose and shape the material, and the people involved in the shaping are also the performers, you have now formed what I would call a devising ensemble.

Ensembles can form for one project and disband, or form a permanent union that requires organization, a name, and a public identity. Actors, directors, writers, and designers typically form the collaborative core that sets the aesthetic tone of the work. In the professional world, new ensembles spring up in both urban and rural areas. They often work out of borrowed spaces or shared studios. They usually produce their first shows in other people's venues, as opposed to owning their own facilities. As they become better established, they frequently tour their work to festivals and mainstream theaters, sometimes developing new performance venues in spaces that have never hosted a show. Some ensembles last for decades, others fade after a year or two.

Professional ensembles

Ensemble work usually begins with a gathering of actors, a hunch, and a desire to create together. Often there is no space, no money, and no separation of tasks. It's a much more disorienting and intuitive way of working than starting from a script, and it requires a unique set of skills. That's what this book is about – developing material collaboratively from beginning process to finished product. Patience, comfort with chaos, willingness to think outside the box, physical risk, creative joy, and non-literal/non-linear thinking are some of the skills this book hopes to encourage. Obviously, this is not a comprehensive survey. There are as many different ways to work as there are companies devising around the world. Some groups use a specific methodology. Some have no shared technique but are unified in their mission, such as giving voice to incarcerated populations or developing documentary theater projects. Some have a clear mission supporting the artistic vision of their founding director; others develop work through collective debate.

A common denominator of many ensembles, from early groups like the Open Theater and the San Francisco Mime Troupe to the 300+ current members of the Network of Ensemble Theaters, is their reliance on bold physical acting styles. Devised performances rarely rely solely on dramatic realism. Ensemble actors tend to be durable and flexible collaborators, comfortable working on material without a roadmap. They are used to working in unorthodox ways. They are as likely to use dance phrases, abstract gesture, song, puppetry, video, and design elements as narratives rather than scripts. Actors in this environment need a healthy dose of patience, intelligence, and goodwill. They need to be willing to make fools of themselves, and to be honest when something doesn't work.

Creating an ensemble piece is not like writing a play (though there *are* devising ensembles who work with writers from the get-go, a good method for avoiding certain creative headaches). It's more like going to the gym to work out. The work begins by getting a group of people together in a room, figuring out what the piece will be about, bouncing ideas around, and developing and editing material. It is a form of writing, but it doesn't begin at the desk of a writer on a pad of paper or on a laptop in silence. It starts in the studio. It starts with people arguing, laughing, drinking, talking, throwing ideas up against the wall and seeing what sticks. It starts by grabbing another person and carrying them upside down while doing an improvised monolog, or picking up a bamboo pole with two other people and trying to express something inexpressible. It continues after rehearsal around the dinner table, in the car, or on a walk as ideas, words, themes, and conflicts are tossed back and forth like volleyballs.

Everyone trained at the Ecole Jacques Lecoq in Paris knows how important discussion over a meal was *après* workshop at the café next door, Chez Jeannette. Devising requires numerous brainstorms and disagreements to achieve an understanding of the limits on a piece and how those limits can generate solutions that surprise and delight. Devising must be built in an atmosphere of trust and mutual respect, or the group will implode. It can be led by a director, writer, composer, or choreographer, or grow out of a complicated group dynamic. Regardless of whether you have two days or two years to produce something, at its core ensemble work exists as a dynamic collaborative process that gives everyone a chance to contribute to a living, organic work of art.

Some ensemble rehearsals resemble jazz jam sessions. When musicians get together, they toss ideas around by improvising melodies, themes, rhythms, and harmonies. Someone proposes an idea and others bend, twist, embellish, and enliven all of its possibilities. Actors in an ensemble typically play off of each other using themselves as the instruments – listening, joining in, holding back, or starting a new theme when the current one is played out. These jam sessions can focus on the topic of a show, on developing technical skills, or on deciding what the topic will be. As a show develops, later rehearsals become more structured. A path is decided on, a writer may be brought in to notate or write dialogue, a roadmap or manifesto is created, research is shared, and the weeks available for making the show are parceled out proportionally to all aspects of the production as the shape of the show becomes clear.

Academic models

Many American colleges are starting to expose students to the devising process. The artistic freedom, the people skills, the problem-solving skills, the leadership challenges, and the ability to think critically and focus ideas are rapidly becoming a valued part of undergraduate training and professional preparation for the theater (and other careers). In business and in science, the ability to work in groups, to find innovative solutions, and to think outside the box are highly valued skills. Training for ensemble work focuses on interaction, intuition, dramaturgy, awareness of others, and collaborative skills. Actors have to plunge deeply into the creative process with a shared commitment to the group's core focus and a willingness to negotiate with others. Ensembles in academia form in courses on ensemble devising for devised class projects, for workshops, and for semester-long projects. Sometimes there are student organizations doing original work. Some schools hire guest artists specializing in devised work for a semester or two to create work with students. Schools teaching ensemble work often include ensemble-devised productions in their seasons. Theater programs teach ensemble theory and practice to prepare students for independent work. Finished performance pieces have the potential to transfer from college to the professional world as students graduate. This training helps develop artistic autonomy and gives students a creative alternative to the traditional model of looking for work individually in repertory theaters. The American company PigPen Theater[2] was formed by theater students who met as freshmen at Carnegie Mellon University, where they began playing music and writing material together, a process that carried over upon graduating to their work as a professional devising ensemble.

Teaching ensemble work

Ensemble devising is an unwieldy topic to teach, with no one accepted methodology and few written texts to guide the work. That's why I wrote this book. Led poorly, an ensemble-devising class can be a disastrous educational experience that will convince participants they should never work this way again. This is usually the result of a teacher or director with little practical experience giving an ensemble too many choices and not enough limits. Groups should start with small, manageable assignments that build confidence and communication skills before tackling major assignments. Teachers and directors should try to get some hands-on training in workshops with professionals before introducing the subject to beginners. If you are starting an ensemble or teaching devising for the first time, start with Fundamentals (Chapter 2) and spend time developing the company's "core" strength, balance, and awareness skills, then move on to Short and Large Prompts (Chapters 3 and 4, respectively). If you already have an existing ensemble, then look at the chapters on Large Prompts (Chapter 4) and Full-Length Pieces (Chapter 6) for ideas you may not have considered.

If you are a teacher or director in a liberal arts college with some experience in ensemble devising and are feeling brave, you may try leading a performance-based project as a class experiment. This can be risky, because students have multiple commitments to other courses and a devised show demands a lot of time. The most you will likely rehearse in one semester is eight to ten weeks, unless you spend a year on the piece. My next devising project with Bowdoin College undergraduates has six weeks from start to finish, so we have a clear mission. The project is design-based. We have the opportunity to work with lighting designer Chris Akerlind for a month-long residency exploring how light affects meaning. Our theme is Light/Dark, and all of the text, poetry, music, object theater, and choreography will be developed by the students in that short period of time. We have two weeks to brainstorm material and work with a puppeteer before Chris arrives. Our goal is to create an immersive environment in a blackbox theater and give the audience a visceral experience of the power of light and darkness in conversation with text, space, and movement.

That's about it. The only other prep we've done is a few technical conversations, and cast a group of experienced actors with musical, design, dramaturgical, and dance backgrounds who like to experiment.

Keep expectations realistic. If you market a devised show as part of the season, let people know the experimental nature of the piece so that you don't box yourselves in with expectations of trying to create something brilliant and important. This will put too much pressure on the experimenting phase of development. If time is short you want to make sure an atmosphere of trust, exploration, and creativity remains at the forefront of your reason for devising the show. I know Chris and I both work quickly as project leaders and are comfortable exploring the unknown. We both are doing this because we want to see what the students will come up with, not use it as a platform for our own work. Their ownership of the piece is one of the real academic values of doing this kind of work. When a teacher, director, or writer says they want to do a devised piece, but take control of all elements early on and turn it into an ego-driven project using the students as puppets to serve out their own personal "vision", it becomes a less productive academic model and will probably send students running from any future devising opportunities. The teaching and leading should come in how time is managed, how prompts are parceled out, how the work gets organized, and in keeping everyone motivated to make their best work possible.

Skills

No matter what type of work you make, skills are needed to give your ideas power and clarity. Art involves making choices and creating an aesthetic experience worth sharing, something requiring thought and skill in its execution. And it must be more than just a technical showcase of skills. It needs to communicate something of value to an audience. Most ensembles do this through a performance vocabulary or training method that gives the work shape and focus. Some groups form after meeting in a workshop or training program where they have learned a shared language. Some develop an aesthetic by copying other groups. Some use a specific movement system. Others follow one visionary leader.

Whatever language your group speaks, once formed you must move beyond the commonality of shared technique to a deep connection to the needs of the audience you want to reach and your goals as artists. The work must grapple with deeply felt ideas, artfully expressed. Good work must be *about* something or it becomes a private experience shared only by others who appreciate that group. Contact improvisation is a useful movement tool, but a fairly boring performance form on its own. A puppeteer can be an excellent designer or manipulator, but their work will be hollow if they have nothing to say other than to display well-made objects in motion.

Content

Examples of ensembles with technique and something to say include British companies like Kneehigh and Punchdrunk. Their productions are not at all alike, but they both use athletic movement and contact improvisation, scenic and verbal skills, to make work that is about something. Neither company relies solely on ensemble devising: they both work with visionary writers, directors, or designers. But their work provides a model for how ensembles can use physical techniques to create something original and compelling. The brilliant reimagining of Henrik Ibsen's *A Doll's House* into *Dollhouse* by the American director Lee Breuer and his company Mabou Mines[3] was full of skillful invention. Puppetry, stilt work, masks, melodrama, live music, and heightened physicality were some of the technical skills applied brilliantly to the heart of the play, a tour de force of shared technique in service to a great idea. Conceived by Lee and adapted by Breuer and Maude Mitchell from Ibsen's original script, I mention it as a model for how far one can also go when reimagining a scripted work for a contemporary audience while remaining true to its essential content.

Whatever skills you employ, I think it is helpful not to have too rigid an idea of what the final work will become. Allow for growth, surprises, promising starts which lead to dead-ends, and so on. Creating an original piece or adaptation is by its nature a series of open-ended challenges. Develop solutions with a roadmap in mind, but never fall too in love with any particular phrase, idea, piece of music, or design concept until it's time for polishing. One thing many ensembles share is a long gestation period. Creating an original show typically demands a long rehearsal process (although brilliant work can be made on short notice as well). Devising usually requires a period of time to develop an idea, a period of time to develop the expressive techniques, and a period of time to workshop, test-run, design, build, and polish the show for the public. This can involve weeks, months, and in some cases, years.

Legacy

A common feature of ensemble work is that the people who do the creating often do the performing. Usually it is a show that no one has done before or will ever do again, a show that lives and dies with the people who created it. Rarely is it written down and passed on to other companies. The unique staging, the characters, the time and place that were a part of making the work; all disappear with that group unless it was taped, digitized, or published. There is no afterlife for it other than the collective memory of the audiences who saw it and the artists who made it. It is a lovely, ephemeral art. Its main legacy is the next generation of artists who make new work based on what went before. And it has grown into an international movement with its own moniker – devising – that is entering mainstream theater as an accepted pedagogical approach and an alternative to doing traditionally scripted shows. I write this book in part to document some of these methods of creation and to encourage others to take the plunge.

2 *Fundamentals*

A well-made house requires skilled carpenters who can read a blueprint; who know how to use power tools and hand tools, how to cut a straight line or a curve, how to make a joint at a complex angle, how to sand and finish – in short, how to build a structure that won't fall down and that is aesthetically pleasing. You also need someone to design the building and produce a ground plan for everyone to follow. All of these skills have parallels in ensemble theater making. Good carpenters don't just bang pieces of wood together with a few nails and hope for the best. Good collaborators know how to move together, listen to each other, and develop and support a shared vision of where they are going. Skilled designers in both fields guide the work. Good architects must consider foundations, siting, weather, materials, longevity, engineering stresses, and internal functionality, as well as aesthetic details, when designing a house. Ensembles have their own parallel version of these same challenges. And both areas need to know when to call in their relevant specialists – plumbers and electricians in the building trades, combat choreographers and lighting designers in the theater world.

This chapter focuses on enhancing the individual actor's abilities to work in an ensemble: their "carpentry" skills, if you will. Later chapters address the design and blueprint challenges actors, directors, writers, and designers solve collaboratively when devising. Every actor in an ensemble needs a sense of balance, alignment, and an understanding of their own strengths and weaknesses, since they are the building blocks that form the material for any ensemble piece. They should be willing to take emotional and physical risks, with an understanding that personal failure and vulnerability are a necessary part of the process of building something new. Time spent in the studio working on personal and ensemble skills will help any group build a more successful piece. Actors who try to do ensemble work with rigid individual needs they have yet to confront, or unresolved issues that chronically pull a group in a negative direction, need to be made aware of their habits before entering the tumultuous world of devising. No one is perfect; flaws are often the root of some of the best material. But a generosity of spirit and ability to take and give feedback objectively is mandatory for all.

The following are exercises I find useful for making work – with students, strangers, and members of my own company. I use these exercises early on in a rehearsal, and return to them as needed later in the process. These are the scales, the nuts and bolts, the mechanical elements of individual and group action needed for clarity and precision in performance. Ballet dancers warm up at the barré with pliés and footwork, musicians practice their scales. Carpenters apprentice with other carpenters. Actors in an ensemble exercise their instruments by developing a common rehearsal language and training together. Many of the skills and techniques mentioned in this chapter are discussed in depth in other books, which I reference in the Appendix. There are exercises here from Jacques Lecoq, Tony Montanaro, the dance troupe Pilobolus, Jerzy Grotowski, Ruth Maleczech, and various dance and theater workshops I've taken over the years. Some are of my own invention. They work equally in the rehearsal hall or the classroom.

You may also need to hire experts for training in areas not mentioned in this chapter. The nature of the piece you are creating will inform your daily process. If you are using Bunraku puppetry or tap dance, take the time to learn them well. When Frantic Assembly staged Bryony Lavery's *Beautiful Burnout* in 2010, their rehearsal process incorporated boxing training. Devote rehearsal time to the skills you need for the story you want to tell from the people who can train you. If there is singing involved, hire a vocal coach. Sloppy work should be a choice, not an overlooked detail. All this training may develop skills that don't directly appear in your finished piece, but the influence of shared training will be felt in the unity of the ensemble's finished work regardless. In some cases, you may just want to hire a specialist to be in the show if training others seems impossible.

Weight work

Weight doesn't lie. It's a wonderful place to start your training because it is rooted in truth. You either carry your weight in front of you, to the back of you, or somewhere towards center. Weight always compensates and always goes somewhere, no matter how complicated your own personal alignment patterns. If you share weight with someone else in a lift, carry, or lean, it all goes somewhere real and observable. It is also very trainable. When you work with other people, the ability to give your weight to (or support) other people is very useful. It is as basic to theater as hammering a nail is to carpentry. Knowing how to find the best and safest way to use the human skeleton as a support, a slingshot, a mitt, or a form that can be rigid or fluid when need be will greatly enhance the expressive range of your work. Metaphorically speaking, you can do the same thing with the material you create: see if it can handle real weight and pressure without collapsing. Individually, these skills can be extended to the gymnastic level with handstands, cartwheels, or tightrope walking. More importantly, when working with other people you open up the door to richer physical imagery as a group, with greater expressive range and the ability to embody natural and man-made phenomena in concert with or in contrast to the text or imagery you are creating. Weight work is one of the main tools I use to produce a broad variety of work, from comic to tragic. It is a fluid and ever-evolving pedagogy that you should feel free to adapt to your own purposes.

Begin with making people aware of the way they use weight – how they personally carry themselves in real life – and how that affects their impulses.

Weight forward

Action
Lean forward over your feet while standing. This is what I call having your weight "on the frontside". From this position, you can do any action: walk, sit, run, lie down even. The point is that by consciously moving your weight to the front, everything is affected. You think differently, you feel differently, your breathing changes, and your use of language is affected.

Variations
It is very important when doing this kind of self-awareness exercise that you work all of the variables. Do not settle into believing it's a "good" or "bad" way to be. Positive and negative feelings can be stirred up by any position; explore both. And actors need to try all speeds, and all degrees of intensity. Once you have found this in the extreme, try experiencing the most minimal degree you can manage and still be aware that your weight is forward of your center of gravity.

Tips
Check in with everyone after working this state for five minutes. What did they experience? How did they feel? What happened to their breathing? How much space were they aware of? What happened to their language center?

Weight on the backside

Action
Do all of the actions you did before, only now, place your weight behind you. Suddenly sitting up is harder, plopping into a chair is

more likely, running feels quite different, but again, side-coach people to feel the positive and negative side to this state, slow and fast, maximum and minimum degrees.

Weight centered

Action

Last but not least, see how it feels to "balance" your weight perfectly, always centered wherever you go, whether running, walking, sitting, and so on. It may start to feel a bit like an Alexander Technique[1] class at this point, which is fine. Still go through all the variations, and then check in at the end on what people experienced.

Counterbalance

This is an exciting movement practice found in gymnastics, dance, and theater. Counterbalance is a natural impulse that can be seen in the daily play of children. It can also be fine-tuned into a high art. I learned some of these techniques from Jonathan Wolken of the dance troupe Pilobolus,[2] which uses counterbalance as one of their main choreographic tools. It is an easy enough concept for beginners to grasp, and an area with nuance and detail that can take years to master as increasingly complex balance points are shared and discovered. Just be careful as risks increase to have spotters and a safe environment with mats or more experienced movers helping while training. A rudimentary knowledge of counterbalance is very handy for creating environments on stage using just bodies. It also appears in many a devising ensemble's work in some form: for duet dialogue patterns, sudden surprises or transitions as a group moves from one world to the next.

Action

Face your partner and hold both their hands or wrists firmly, with your toes almost touching. Lean away from each other until you share each other's weight. Don't let go, as either of you will fall. Make it a habit to come back up to center and ease your way back out slowly until you can comfortably keep each other balanced without struggling. This is the basic starting position for counterbalancing, where bodies are in a state of balance, like a see-saw sculpture where the feet together serve as one fulcrum.

Tips

Counterbalancing is an active act, not a rigid statue. You both need to keep making small adjustments to stay aligned. Learn to let the position do the work. Make eye contact. Talk to each other. Your arms should be fully extended, shoulders down, so that you aren't trying to "hide" your weight from your partner. Hips should lean away from the center, not hug into it. As you get comfortable staying in balance, you can begin to move, like a mirror, away from the center further. Hips can extend all the way out as you lower yourselves towards the floor, or release one arm and both partners can extend the other arm for balance.

Find the fine line between being too limp and too rigid. Weight work requires a kind of firm but elastic use of the body. You can hold your own weight to a degree so that it is easier for your partner to balance you, but you must also give that gathered weight over to your partner in a manageable form so that they can "feel" where the center is; neither a wobbly bowl of jello (which is hard to handle) or a bundle of tension (which is dangerous; a little massage may be needed first). Both of you want to develop a low, shared center of gravity with relaxed shoulders, long limbs, and a real sense of each other's weight.

Different heights and weights can work well together: they just require more compensation by the smaller person, who needs to lean out further than the larger person. To learn this technique, it is easier to work with someone roughly your size at first, and then move on to handling greater disparities.

If you have a partner who doesn't quite trust you or is afraid of giving you their full weight, try alternating who is the "base" and who is "floating". Have one person who gives up their weight first. As they lean out, the other partner keeps talking to them and reminds them to "give me your weight". Eventually you will find the point at which both of you are fully engaged. Switch who is the base and repeat.

Variations
Once you have mastered this basic facing-front position, try leaning out side by side, back to back, one front and one back, or anchoring other parts of the body. The variations are endless. Work slowly and patiently, finding all of the ways you can lean away from the center and still share weight.

The opposite force is equally useful. Try leaning in rather than leaning out. Lean back to back, creating a shared fulcrum at the center while the other parts of your body work further out to add risk and distance from your shared center. Go back to the principle of a "base" and a "flyer", and give your weight to each other with one working as a base while the other shares their weight in a variety of positions in which they lean into rather than away from their partner. If you work in a larger group, usually someone is always moving with their weight towards the center or from underneath while others are moving away from the center or on top. Do be *careful*! Don't get too fancy and lift your feet at the wrong time – you might roll over into a neck or back injury at the wrong moment. Keep your feet on the ground for a long time, and work with a professional, a dancer, a Contact Improvisation person, or someone else who knows what they are doing before doing anything too advanced. The dance troupe Pilobolus is masterful at this kind of work. Seeing them in performance, or the dance troupe Momix,[3] will give you some idea of what can be done with counterbalance and weight work. Once you have developed sensitivity for working with a partner, merge pairs into quartettes. Find ways to move slowly as a group. When you find a point of equilibrium, evolve that pattern without losing the interdependence, like an organism in motion.

Piggyback rides, wheelbarrows, flying angels (leaning your hips over someone's feet and balancing), all of these children's games are variations on counterbalancing. Often in musical theater you will see a fancy move that is based on sharing weight for a moment, turning it into a lift, a toss, a catch, or a pose. The modern dance troupe led by Elizabeth Streb[4] is known for its explosive use of falling and lifting. I am most interested in how this work can expand dramatic territories to reveal moments of tremendous intimacy or cruelty, surprising beauty or comedy. A theater ensemble that uses weight work with contemporary text is the British troupe Frantic Assembly.[5] The blend of technique and narrative in their work and in shows they have choreographed for others, such as the National Theatre's production of *The Curious Incident of the Dog in the Night-Time* or the National Theatre of Scotland's *Black Watch*, is thrilling. Frantic founders Scott Graham and Steven Hoggett have opened up new directions in theater physicality with their use of weight, gesture, and counterbalance.

Yielding

Another quality that can be tuned up is the ability to "yield" your weight. This helps develop an instinctual understanding of the different percentages of physical tension or ease you have at your control.

Action
Get a partner. Person A is yielding, B is sending forces through their body. Person A stands in alignment/neutral with weight on both feet, low center of gravity. B starts from the backside on the shoulders, making contact first with a palm flat on the shoulder then sending a force through their blade and out the other side. It's a push that meets no resistance, the hand moves past the partner, the partner lets the force escape and returns to neutral. The effect should be like a breeze blowing through that bends a blade of grass momentarily (the shoulder moves to allow the hand to pass through, and then returns).

Tips

Start gently. Don't send huge shock waves through, and don't smack the body in a way that stings. Just place a hand on the shoulder, and push straight through. The Yielder should only move the area affected. If it is a bigger push, it might involve a bit more hip or torso. Pushers should try to alternate degrees of force and vary the shoulders used.

Give your partner a chance to return to neutral each time; don't go so fast that a ripple from the previous shock is still dissipating.

Variations

Start moving around the partner, and sending a force through from the front, the side, through the leg, down like a jack-in-the-box, and so on. Eventually the person yielding should keep returning to neutral with no added tension, and always be available for any force passing through them. Don't anticipate the direction or "help" the person sending the force through. If you guess wrong, you'll know it. Pushers can also usually feel when the Yielder is helping too much, or over-interpreting. Simply obey Newton's Laws of Motion. No more nor less a reaction than the action calls for. Watch out for "echo", a tendency some people have to wobble or bounce after an action. The inverse is also true, pulling back too fast with held energy like a rubber band. You want to think more like a tree, with branches that return effortlessly as soon as the breeze passing through lets up, not an elastic band that snaps back. Person B should vary the timing and direction so that the partner can't predict where the force is coming from. B can also use hips, back, and legs to send a force through their partner, not just hands.

Once you start to get a feel for just the right amount of held energy needed to yield and return to neutral, trade off. Then trade off again, and play a little game of yielding for a bit and then trading control, so that the game moves back and forth with almost every action.

Resistance

The next force learned after yielding is resistance.

Action

Go back to the original yielding exercise, only this time when B sends a force through A's shoulder, A plays with resistance. A can push back after the hand moves through, during the action, or right before the action starts. This is the beginning of a rich dialogue. Just using that same pushing action, see how the "meaning" changes when you vary how quickly or strongly you resist. Immediately your partner will start to feel a dialogue, a little drama of pressure and resistance, yielding and opposing that starts to create a relationship.

Tips

Remember the carpenter metaphor. Work methodically in one area thoroughly before moving onto the next, and make sure your body really "gets" the idea. Just because your shoulder has figured it out doesn't mean your head will. Move around the body, and play with different areas yielding and resisting. Stay with one person as A doing all the resisting and yielding, and B sending all the forces. This can go on for quite a while, as more complex moves evolve using the whole body, with small areas providing some resistance, or larger areas doing some yielding.

Important!

Both people need to know from the outset that safety is rule one. No matter what position you end up in, no one should "trick" the other into falling, losing their balance, or making a poor choice that would hurt their partner. Play vigorously, but develop a level of trust and understanding as you get more active. Always save the other person from injury if needed.

Variations

After both partners have been A and B, go into a dialogue where neither one of you is leading or following. Start working with yielding and resisting, evolving into lifting and carrying, without having to say who is A and who is B. This leads naturally into the next exercise, Driving a sports car.

Driving a sports car

Action

Travel with your partner. I like to think of it as one driver, one Mercedes. A is the sports car, B is steering. The ideal energy to develop is that A is like a finely tuned machine, able to read every signal from B to stop, start, accelerate, slow down, go low, go high, run, or pause. B should *always* stay in physical contact with A, and guide them from the arms, the back, the head, the fingertips, and any other way they can think of. *Watch out* for the other drivers. Again, safety is rule one, drivers must be aware of other people driving, and head for open areas, only turning on the gas and doing something risky when there is room to do it. If two people are heading right for each other, they both should be able to hug/pause/embrace/or sharp turn the sports car to avoid collision. Trade off.

Tips

Watch out for each other's toes. The footwork in this can get tricky, and it is the main source of frustration. Whether you have a light touch as a driver, or a firm grip, the "car" should do its best to follow all cues with no resistance or mind of its own. Some "cars" have a lot of tension in their bodies, and need to be softened up by doing some quick back-and-forths and up-and-downs before traveling very fast.

Variations

While this starts as primarily a "following" exercise for A developing their ability to interpret B's signals, eventually A can add resistance to create more complex patterns. Develop the ability of A to follow first, then add a little independent thinking to the equation. After playing with that for a bit, develop the ability to trade off who is steering and who is following, to the point where both A and B are sometimes moving in unison, sometimes playing with call and response, and sometimes just yielding.

   Once you are both adept at reading each other's signals, and you can tell the difference between yielding and resisting, you also start to develop a knack for when your partner *wants* you to yield or resist. This changes from person to person, and over time you can develop an instinct for what to ask for and when to ask for it. Bottom line, if someone runs at you and leaps in your arms, catch them! Safety should also be rule one. If you are in a room with a few pairs of people, open up the driving options by trading partners. See what happens if you liberate people from the contact rule, and let them fly solo for a bit. If two pairs meet, they can make a quartette, form new duos, or create four solos. Start treating the whole room like a molecular dance with temporary partnerships playing out. Embrace conflict, too: you can change and be changed by what the other person does, and by how you feel about your own actions with others. Vary your levels. Vary intensity. If you find an interesting moment or relationship, explore it fully, then move on. When in doubt, pause, but stay alive internally, and look for where you want to go next.

   Ruth Malazchek and Sharon Fogarty from Mabou Mines[6] led a workshop on their company's methods at Amherst College a few years back, and I remember vividly their use of a basic rule of three when doing any impulse explorations, whether solo or with others. Go after an impulse, go after it again, and then find satisfaction by putting your all into the third try. If you can't find expressive satisfaction after three attempts, move on. Carry out little physical conversations by offering to give or take weight on contact and in the moment, but *no dialogue*! You can use music while doing this, make open sounds and noises, but don't cut the interplay short by trying to force a verbal plot on top of the impulsive work. Work at an animal level of action and reaction. Be noisy, but stay out of your head. Be aware of things getting too chaotic or out of control and the risk of injury getting too great. Slow down or pause when needed.

Time

Time is another variable that affects our behavior. Some people are colored by an event from the past – recent, distant, or chronic. We are pulled by time, pushed by time, or frozen by it, with almost as much palpable force as our attraction and repulsion to people. Some are anticipating events in the future, eagerly or with dread. Sometimes we are living right in the moment, especially when having an intense experience like a roller coaster ride that leaves no room for experiencing anything else. This hidden sense of what "time" we inhabit is an important component in understanding where our weight and focus is. This is a different variable to consider than the concept of tempo or speed applied to any action. This is more about an internal state of being that colors all actions.

Colored by the past

Action
Pick something specific, real or imagined, that happened in the past and allow it to dominate your thinking and feeling. It can be as recent as a few minutes ago – something someone said, something you just remembered, something that actually happened that morning – or it can be from weeks or years ago – the anniversary of a loved one dying, a vivid memory of someone who hurt you. Just make sure it is something that can really trigger your imagination, so that you don't have to work at it affecting you. Just let it be there, and then go on about your business. Walk, run, stand, talk to other people in the room, and just let the past color your present without feeling the need to tell anyone what it is that is really affecting you. Keep it secret, as we often do in life. Whatever you are using to trigger your behavior, it is private: its effect is public. This is where the line between good theater and drama therapy is drawn. Even if you want to tell other people what is affecting you, it really isn't part of this exercise: keep it to yourself.

After five minutes of doing this, come back to the present fully and share what you experienced, what you noticed about the other people in the room and in yourself. What happened to focus, to breathing, to weight, to your energy, and sense of space?

Variations
Do the same thing with Living in The Future, and then Living in The Present. Spend five minutes in each state, and discuss the differences. With The Future, it can be something you are about to do right after class, after rehearsal, something you are planning to do later on that week: again, anything real or imagined that works as a powerful trigger for your behavior.

You can also repeat the exercise with any of these states and make a different choice from the first time through. For example, if you picked something you feared was about to happen, try expecting something joyous. If you were excited by what happened that morning, try being affected by something dreadful that happened, real or imagined. Hopefully, after consciously playing with each of these states, with personal space, and with where your focus and weight are at a given time, you will begin to tune your awareness of self and others. This should give you the ability to more quickly find a balanced, available state of presence, a readiness for all. If you can become a player who is less a creature of habitual movement patterns, someone able to adapt to any given situation or imagined event, you will have a better base for making work.

Tempo variations

Action

Think of all action as moving from the slowest to the fastest on a scale of one to ten. Choose an activity, or simply do a little walking through the space as a group, but vary the tempo. Have an outside person call out numbers at random, and shift gears accordingly. Start out gradually. At speed one, the movement is imperceptible. Pick up the pace through each number, hitting mid-speed at five, and full throttle at ten. Then play with contrasts. Go from ten to two to nine then five, and vary the pace at which the numbers are called out.

Variations

Any solo action, monologue, or duet scene can be explored by varying the tempo to change the meaning. Begin a scene or activity or monologue, and have an outside person call "Change!" at any time. Actor(s) must shift tempo immediately, and explore the new meaning that is found by going faster or slower or pausing. Change can also mean one person goes faster while the other slower; they do not need to match tempos.

Rhythm

It is essential in any ensemble that every actor can "feel the beat". Rhythm is a primal force that bonds people in every situation. Make sure everyone can hear the same beat. Develop the group's ability to play on the downbeat, the offbeat, the suspended rests, and with syncopation. I'm going to describe a few exercises I use a lot. My apologies if you invented this and do it differently. I don't know all the origins. Do make these your own as you work with them. The first couple of exercises are from Jacques Lecoq.

Clapping

Action

Two people face each other. With hands in front of you, shoulder width apart, person A claps on the downbeat (1–3–5–7) at a steady, moderate pace. person B holds their hands perpendicular to A and claps on the backbeat (2–4–6–8), landing the clap in the center of person A's clapping pattern, but avoiding getting hit by A because they are clapping in syncopation. Done correctly, it looks like a two-stroke engine, with pistons crossing but never hitting. Both keep the same pace, and person B practices matching the clapping of person A by mirroring them, then pausing for a beat and half to go back to the counterpoint, or jumping a half-beat to get the claps to intersect. Trade off who holds the downbeat, and let the other person try to find how to fit the offbeat in.

Rhythmic walking

Action

This same experience of rhythm can be done while walking. When we walk, we fall into a pattern that accents the downbeat. Take a walk and count your steps out loud with eight beats, and you will find your walk fits well into 1–3–5–7 as a natural rhythm. You can also walk on the backbeat, which means count out loud and step on the 2–4–6–8 instead. It is exactly the same walk, but done with a different rhythmic awareness. Now work with another person, and see if you can (starting slowly!) put the two steps together so that you are walking side by side in unison on the 1–3–5–7, and then have one person hesitate a beat and a half or jump the beat, and walk with one person on the downbeat and one on the backbeat. It can be done. Don't change the tempo.

Lecoq always looked for the dramatic transposition of these underlying principles in life, and would advise us that once we had found the pattern, try to carry on a conversation, with two people listening to each other but holding onto their separate agendas, like priests or ministers going for a walk and discussing a problem. Notice how the dialogue and mood changes when they are "in step" or "out of step".

3 over 4

Action

Another example of using rhythm with different accents that can be quite a challenge, but that helps expand the sensitivity of any performer, is the ability to play 3 over 4 at the same time. In other words, you can slap your right knee on a steady four count, going

1–2–3–4, while hitting the other knee on a three count, always accenting the one as the downbeat. If you do it with another person (one does the three count, the other the four) it's easier to hear. The person doing 1–2–3 always accents the one, the person doing four does the same. The person doing three will accent their one on the other person's four, then three, then two, and back to a shared one after four rounds. Then try it alone, by counting and accenting the first beat of three each time. It will go 123, 412, 341, 234, and back to 1 as a shared accent.

Mabou Mines reductions

This was an exercise I learned from Ruth Malezchek that Phillip Glass did with Mabou Mines when he was a company member.

Action
Form two lines. One group says the even numbers, one group says the odd. Alternate sides so that group A says one, group B says two, and so on up to eight, then count back down. Each time you go up the "scale" reduce it by one number, so that it goes like this:

   12345678 – 1234567 – 123456 – 12345 – 1234 – 123 – 12 – 1

Because you are in two groups, every other time you count to the highest number the odd numbers will jump the beat and say two numbers in a row while the evens rest. Try it. It's harder than it sounds. Once the group gets the hang of that, instead of counting, each group sings a note and clicks fingers without saying any numbers, and does the same thing counting internally. It being Phillip Glass, its more interesting if the odd numbers have one tone and the even numbers use another contrasting tone. It takes great focus, but is great fun to do. I have seen groups try for hours and not quit until they can do it perfectly. It's a great way to tune up and take a break from moving for a while so you can focus on musical/rhythmic attunement rather than movement.

Kirtan

Action
A group rhythmic jam. This exercise was developed by Tony Montanaro at the Celebration Barn,[7] based on the idea of spiritual music improvisation found in India. Everyone closes their eyes, gets comfortable, breathes, and listens to the quiet. Then *very* gradually, allow for little noise impulses to begin. Weave a sound fabric with a movement fabric, so that as you begin to make sound, you also start to move. It might just be small breath sounds at first, or whistles and

clucks and small mouth sounds. Keep the group focused on one event, don't digress into separate duos or solos. As people start to move, open your eyes and build the actions along with the sound. It might start as small swaying patterns, or popcorn effect jumps, or a rhythmic stomp of some kind. Each kirtan is completely different.

If the sounds and movements you make are affected by everything you hear, and by the people around you, then it should build as one group, as long as everyone is doing roughly 30% personal impulses, 30% listening, and 40% contributing to the whole as it grows. It can get quite vigorous, with people banging on the walls, chairs, and the floor as a percussion instrument, and tribal movement patterns developing spontaneously that everyone can follow organically without thinking about it. As the musician Herbie Hancock[8] once said in a radio interview talking about music improvisation, it is like the Buddhist idea of "many in body, one in mind". Let the improvisation grow and shrink, until it finds a natural ending. You may need an outside eye to coach it or pronounce it finished, as they do tend to just keep going; 15–20 minutes is a good length for one round.

1 and 2 and 3 . . .

Action

Start by playing what Viola Spolin[9] (author of *Improvisation for the Theater*) calls "Lone Wolf". Everyone stands still throughout the space, then someone starts moving around the room. The game is to only have one person moving at a time – but always have someone moving. At any time, someone else can take the lead and start moving. The previous person moving must instantly stop. If no one cuts in, the current person just keeps moving. If two people start at the same time, one has to stop.

Tip

Take the lead when the current "mover" can hear or see you, to get the hang of it. Then vary the timing, trade off more rapidly, and so on.

Variation

To turn Lone Wolf into one then two then three . . . start by having one person move, pause, then two people move, pause, and so on. Let's say you have ten people. Person 1 moves, everyone else is still. Then 1 stops on their own. Now two people start together, and only those two should move. Then they *both* stop at the same time. Pause. Now three people start at the same moment until all three see the moment to pause together. Do this all the way up to ten if you can. If more people start moving than the correct number, or if not enough start moving, then that round is over and you go back to the beginning and start with one. It's infuriating at first, but I have seen most groups make it to level six or seven without too much difficulty, which is very satisfying. It is almost a skill in ESP as much as spatial awareness, a feel for the "right" moment, trust in the group, acting on an impulse, and other intangible qualities.

Many people do a version of this as a verbal counting game by counting to ten without picking an order in advance. One person says the number one, then someone says two, and so on. You don't all need to say a number. One person can say more numbers than another. You must speak when no one else does, and if two people say the same number at the same time, you have to start over. The value in both exercises is a state of listening.

Space

Personal space

Action

Put one actor in the center of four others. Have them stand at four compass points facing the actor in the middle, with the actor in the middle facing front at one of the actors who is "north". Using hand gestures, the person in the center waves people closer in or further away by inches and millimeters until they can place them exactly on the boundary of their comfort zone, that point at which they do not feel their space is being "invaded" by the other actors. The front one is the easiest, because they are facing you straight on, and you will have a visceral feeling of when they are "too close". The side ones are just done with peripheral vision, and are a bit harder to "feel". The actor in the center cannot turn to look at them. And the back one is pure intuition, using hand signals; it's just a feeling of when you are "safe". Once they are finished placing people, step out of the center and see what you "drew". That is the outline of your personal space.

Once each actor has taken a turn and become more aware of their sense of personal space, practice as a group, but still working solo, these other variables that affect our behavior and our physical relationship to the world.

Stretch space

Action

Get with a partner. Stay in eye contact. Create a bond of energy between you, a relationship in space that nothing can puncture. Now stretch the space between you without losing the feeling that the two of you are "connected". If either of you feels the chemistry is weak, get closer to each other and re-establish the bond. Do this without dialogue at first.

Tips

Pay no attention to the other pairs working in the room, other than to make sure you don't step on anyone or slam into someone. You should work to the maximum distance apart that the two of you can stretch and still maintain a sense of connection. In a theater, this could go as far as one person out in the rear balcony and one person against the upstage wall. Just be honest about your sense of connection. Anyone slipping must re-find it. And be sure you get quite close. Use levels, use the floor, move with a variety of tempos. Make all of your actions call and response to each other. Add gestures, breathe, vary the tempo, play with stillness as well.

Variations

Once you've played with stretching the space in silence, you can add a bit of sound or language. Play out individual moments of impulse vocally as needed. Don't plot or be clever, just let the situation carry you, and when language is needed, use it and respond to your partner's use of it.

Field of vision

Everyone has a personal habit of where they focus, just as they have habits of where their weight is carried. Even though focus shifts with different tasks, left on your own when walking down a street you tend to fall into one of these broad categories. It's a good idea to try all of them purposefully, and become masterful at doing any one as needed. Allow the focus to completely change the way you breathe, think, feel, and move through space. These exercises came in some form from the Ecole Jacques Lecoq.

Action

Spend four to five minutes walking, running, sitting, and standing with a very specific point of focus that is *narrow* and *direct*. *Always* look right at something, and allow it to affect your psychology, your breathing, your relationship to the room, and all the others in it. Explore space and respond to stimulus by always maintaining this narrow, direct focus. Think of it as moving like a horse with blinders on. Do not shift your focus or allow your eyes to wander. *Always* have a specific point of focus. Move towards it or away from it or be still. Use your arms to amplify the experience, holding them out in front of you parallel to each other like giant blinders. When it is time to look elsewhere, do so with no hesitation or ambiguity. Be direct and clear with your focus; see how your mind and body responds. As always, remember to explore all variables: slow–fast, light–dark, fear–joy, and so on. Reflect afterwards on what you discovered: how your breathing changed, what mood it put you in, what kind of words you were able to speak; share your reactions with others.

Variations

Do the same using other typical fields of vision. Try a *high diagonal focus*, always looking up at 45 degrees, using your voice to explore the thoughts and feelings you can, never looking down at other people or the horizon. Try *low diagonal*, looking at the ground out in front of you at a 45-degree angle as you move. Use the arms on all of these planes to remind you of what the focus is, then put them down. Try a *wide focus*, taking in as much of the space and others as you can at all times. Try a *shallow focus*, as if you were looking at something a foot away from your nose, with a soft blur – that place we go to when daydreaming, thinking about something else, "spacing out". Then try a *scattered focus*, moving from direct, to diagonal, to unfocused in a random pattern. Stay within the limits of each "point of focus" for three to four minutes. Now notice your own patterns. Is it clearer what your own default pattern is?

Floor patterns

Action

In a group of seven to eight, move through the space using floor patterns that are called out. Have an outside person say "circle", and everyone move in a floor pattern that is circular. People can move at different tempos and different-sized circles. Stay aware of the space and each other; if a collision is about to occur, slow down, speed up, or pause. The outside caller can switch to squares, straight lines, triangles, any floor pattern they choose. Allow for interaction, and be affected by the other people moving to make choices. Build patterns, relationships, and moments of aggression or playfulness as part of the improvisation.

Variations

Combine different patterns. Split into three groups: A does circles, B does squares, and C does triangles. The outside person calls "switch", and every group chooses a new pattern. Work the space and weave relationships with others as you travel.

Try it as three choral groups, moving as a clump in a given floor pattern, not individuals making circles, squares, or triangles.

Personal walks

Action

Walk throughout the space, and have someone call out variations on what part of the body is leading the walk. Try someone who leads from the head, or the hips, or who walks with wide-open arms or a constricted chest cavity. Notice what part of the foot you put your weight on. Try all variations such as landing on toes first, landing heel first, quiet on your feet, stomping, gliding, landing on the outside of the arch, knock-kneed, fast rhythms, slow, etc.

Variations

Notice how visual focus affects your movements. Walk while practicing the Fields of Vision exercise described above. Do the same thing by walking with a Past–Present–Future inner focus, and notice how that affects your walk. Once you have done these exercises, apply them to a real analysis of your own movement patterns. The following exercise from the Lecoq school[10] increases your awareness of personal movement patterns and the subconscious choices affecting gaits at any given moment.

Copying walks

Action

Get a partner. Spend five minutes following them around the room, mimic their walk as accurately as possible. Where do they put their weight, where do they hold tension? Match their pace exactly. What is their point of view? Try to watch them from the front, and see how much space they are aware of, what seems to be going on inside their head when they walk. Trade off, and spend five minutes with your partner learning your walk. Once everyone has learned someone's walk, stand in a large circle and have one pair go first. Person A follows person B, and gets an accurate match going with outside coaching from the circle pointing out any details or variations that can be fine-tuned. Once the match is accurate, the "original" person steps out, and watches from outside to see what their walk looks like with someone else "doing" their walk.

This is a very useful exercise for developing sensitivity to other people's ways of being. It helps actors break out of their own rhythms and into someone else's point of view. Small changes can make a huge impact, and a group of people observing actors doing this work can quickly spot when a walk "matches" and the actors have done a good job of fully inhabiting someone else's world. It is also very humbling to see what you look like from the outside, what habits and adjustments another person has to make when they play you. You can never become another person on stage without first understanding the habits you have, and how the world perceives you. Lecoq also uses this exercise to prepare people for neutral mask work, making people more aware of their personal habits and patterns and steering them towards a more neutral starting point.

Follow the leader

One person crosses the room, everyone else follows them copying their gesture, action, rhythm. A good way to warm up.

Variations

There are many versions. A nice choral exercise is to appoint a leader, follow them for a couple of actions, and then allow the next logical person to take charge. An outside person can call out different leaders to get it started, and then allow the group to sense when the leadership should change, and instantly follow that new person.

Group exercises

Milling and seething

There are endless variations on this simple group warm-up. It can be done with music, or without. The basic idea is to have everyone walk at a good speed with minimal tension, looking for and moving towards open spaces in the room and between each other, keeping their eyes on the horizon so that they see the space and the other players. Like atoms circulating and redistributing through space. When collisions occur, try to make them soft and use the other person to change direction and keep moving.

Variations

Try using different speeds, with one being the slowest setting and ten the highest. Have a leader call out which "gear" you are in, making sure that the group doesn't get out of control.

Side-coach people to try using the floor, use gesture patterns, copy something you see in other people, play little games rhythmically with others, join in with an event, and then move on when it bores you. Make sure you alternate offering to lead an event with at other times following others.

Use floor patterns as the basic walk–run variation, starting with circles, then triangles, then squares, and so on. Subdivide the groups into circling people, triangular people, and straight line people. Keep using tempo and awareness to pick up the speed and challenge the group to work to its maximum and minimum capabilities.

Rounds

Action

Get into groups of five to six. One person gets up and, facing the group, does a short sound and movement pattern, playing off of whatever mood or impulse strikes them at that moment. They repeat it a couple of times to strengthen and clarify its rhythm, meaning, and feeling, and then sit back down. The next person to go is whoever has an "impulse" to jump up and express something. They can do something completely different, or be somehow affected by the previous person's sound and movement. It is best not to go around in a predictable order, because people tend to start planning their actions or responses. Go when the mood strikes. Someone can go twice in a row if they like, just make sure you do all jump up several times. This is a very good exercise for developing individual impulsiveness that was developed by Tony Montanaro at the Celebration Barn Theater.

Variations
Try Rounds on a theme. Choose a topic for the group to jam on (i.e., War, Summertime, Divorce, Betrayal, Work), and without comment or judgment, let that theme influence every impulse to move or make sound. Start to allow language in the moments, so that they grow in depth and complexity. Try call and response, so that another person can jump in and join someone else's impulse by adding their own action and sound when they see/feel a need.

Tips
Make sure it doesn't bog down into a lengthy scene; keep using Rounds to test ideas and movements that you can polish and return to later. In the early stages, just keep going, even if it means long pauses between people after all of the obvious ideas and actions have been exhausted. That's when the richer material starts to surface, and deeper imagery begins to show up. Stare at the empty stage until someone gets up and does something.

Whoosh!

Sound and movement exercises in a circle come in many forms. The earliest versions I know of came from voice teacher Kristin Linklater's[11] work to connect body and voice with the Open Theater back in the 1960s. There are versions where you pass a gesture to the person on your right and they transform it, versions where one person does a sound and movement twice, then everyone repeats it. There is Zip–Zap–Zop, Rabbit–Elephant–1776, circles with balls tossed to someone in the center or around the edge, circles using names and numbers. Whoosh! is my current favorite for getting everyone energized and focused. It is a great exercise for developing full-bodied commitment to gestures and an awareness of connecting to everyone in the room. I learned this version from a touring theater ensemble called Wakka Wakka,[12] a touring group that met at the Lecoq school. I have since run into many other versions.

Action
Stand in a circle, weight grounded, ready for anything. One person starts an action with a gesture and sound that is passed around the circle with clarity, vigor, and speed. The goal is to pass the sound and movement quickly and smoothly, while staying alert to the variations

so that you do not move or speak unless you are supposed to. There are several "commands" to learn.

- *Whiz*! Tosses energy sideways. First person goes *"whiz!"* in one direction, swinging both arms with full energy in one direction towards the person next to them, who passes it on. Go around the circle in the same direction for a while, until everyone is fully committed to the sound and gesture using their whole body with their hips, arms, and eye contact passing energy while saying *"whiz!"* A good ensemble can send it around seamlessly with no bumps or pauses at a very brisk clip, as if a breeze blew one sound/gesture around the circle. Make a clear, strong gesture sideways towards whoever is next while saying *whiz*!

- *Bong*! Blocks a *whiz*! You can block a *whiz*! by holding your arm up, fist raised, bent elbow, and say *"bong!"* This blocks the *whiz*! and reverses it. The person who sent the *whiz*! must immediately reverse direction and send a *whiz*! the other way. Anyone can go *bong*! instead of whiz at any time and change the direction of the pass.

- *Whoosh*! Tosses across the space. Anyone can make eye contact across the circle to someone and toss the energy across the space with a *whoosh*! Instead of gesturing sideways, you send both arms out like a basketball pass right at someone you make eye contact with while saying *"whoosh!"* They either accept it or reject it by saying:

- *Aaahhh*...Accepts a *whoosh*! If you accept the *whoosh*! swim in it with a full body, sensual delight saying *"aaahhh..."* arms open, leaning back, and shimmying in it a bit like a warm shower spraying over you. Then continue the *whiz*! or *whoosh*! of your choice. If you reject the toss of the *whoosh*!, then you say:

- *Ziggy Ziggy Ziggy*! Blocks a *whoosh*! Make an x with both arms and block the energy of the airborne *whoosh*! coming at you. This means the thrower of the *whoosh*! must do another toss to someone else.

- *Hark*! A free throw for anyone to take. Using one arm, lob the energy up in the air in the center, as if throwing a ball way up in the center while saying *"hark!"* As it "comes down", anyone can grab it but they have to use a:

- *Swipe*! The only way to claim a *hark*! Reach up and grab with one hand, like you were snagging a ring out of the air, and grab the energy of the *hark*! while saying *"swipe!"* If two people say *swipe*! at the same time, they are both out.

These are all the elements of the game, now for the competitive part. Any time someone misses out on the rhythm of a toss or a catch, they are out and must "sit in the soup" (go sit in the center of the circle until the round is over). If two people do a *swipe!* at the same time, they both go in. If a person tosses a *whoosh!* with no receiver in focus, they go in. If you make a mistake passing in direction, timing, or response to any of the actions, you are out of the round and must sit in the soup.

Variations

This is an enormously fun game to play, and very invigorating. I like to play it to warm up a cast before a show, to wake people up in the morning, or to focus everyone's awareness and tune up their reflexes. You don't have to play elimination. You can just keep playing until everyone feels alert. Or if you must make it competitive, take a letter every time you screw up and sit out only if you spell *spud*, so that everyone can get to play longer.

I have seen people add their own variations, with new rules that add to the gestures and words in play.

In Bogotá, Colombia, I learned a version played locally called:

Jah!

Action

Same basic idea of standing in a circle, and passing sound and movements quickly around the circle. There are only four commands in Jah!, but it is played very quickly and develops real spatial awareness and lots of excitement.

- *Jah!* Like Whiz!, you stand in a circle and go very quickly around saying "*jah*" with a diagonal stabbing motion with your arm across your chest and down towards a person to your left or right, passing it in the direction you stab.
- *Hondom!* Reverses the action. Both hands are held up by your ears with fists clenched, elbows bent, as if you were making a gesture like a boxer.
- *Aye!* Both hands go up to the eyes like you were making goggles with your hands. The action skips over the next person to you, and continues in the same direction with the next person deciding what to do.
- *Angel!* Both arms open wide towards the sky, like a prayer. Action reverses, like *hondom!*, only it skips one person, so the next person has to decide what to do.

Row your boat

Another ensemble builder is singing the song "Row, Row, Row Your Boat, Gently Down the Stream. Merrily, Merrily, Merrily, Merrily, Life is but a Dream" in a circle. I use this often each night before a show as part of a vocal warm-up when we are in production. It is also a good exercise early on in rehearsal to build awareness and musicality.

Action

Sing the song once through in unison, then sing it one word per person at a time as it goes around the circle, trying not to break the rhythm of the song. Pass the energy around the circle without dropping the beat or the melody. Feel the pace of it as it comes at you, and link your word with the previous person's word as you send it to the next person. When you get to the end of the verse, sing it all in unison once through, then do another round one word at a time starting as a solo of one word per person where you left off. Continue till all the bumps have been evened out and the group can sing it in unison or one word at a time with the same pace.

Variation

You can do this with any song, or a line of text. A good variation is to change the tone, the volume, and the vocal color of the solo round after you have sung it in unison. The first person to go gives it a new flavor which everyone adopts until that round is completed: elongated vowels, clipped British accents, whispering menacingly, operatic abandon, and so on. Go back to unison normal after the solo round completes the phrase, then start a new vocal/physical choice for the next solo round. After that, try having anyone change it in the circle as it goes around on any solo word, as long as every choice is supported by at least one previous person's choice before a new change is introduced, so that each choice is at least two words long.

If you choose to use a line of text instead of a song, treat it the same way. Choose a line from Shakespeare, for instance "Sleep no more! Macbeth does murder sleep". Say it in unison once, then one word at a time around the circle. Start playing with tone, inflection, and so on.

Qualities of movement

The elements

Lecoq says the two great sources for making theater are the natural world and everyday human behavior (Interview, Physical Comedy Handbook, Robinson, 1999). The four elements – earth, water, air, fire – are a great source for exploring the natural world, and these exercises from the Lecoq school are just the beginning of what is possible. Identifying and moving within each element helps to develop physical expressiveness, and playing with all the variables within each element from calmest to most turbulent is a great workout. Many of these exercises work best in a group, and doing them together helps an ensemble develop better sensitivity to each other, to choral impulses, and to group thinking. Working with the elements often involves finding a *quality* of sound and movement first, and then playing with the *dynamics* by moving from the calmest state to the most energetic within that particular quality, then allowing the energy to subside to a point of stillness again, leaving the actor transformed by their journey.

With each element, start by recognizing the words rooted in that element. Free associate out loud all of the behavioral words associated with that element, mention all the phrases identified with that element. For instance, earth conjures up words like "dirty", "solid", "rocky", "grounded", and "deep", or phrases like "shaken to the core" or "down to earth". "Rooted" itself is also a word that belongs to earth. Air inspires "breathes", "floats", has "gusto", is "full of hot air", is "blustery". The temperature of the element also matters. Water can be a gas, a solid, and a liquid, depending on heat, moving from "icy" stillness to "showers" of joy. As you work with each element, be aware of how the breath changes, the center of gravity shifts, and how your psychological impulses change and different words are provoked by each element. In the Lecoq pedagogy, significant time is spent working with neutral mask first to establish an open and available presence. If there is a good neutral mask teacher in your area, they will also most likely be aware of, and have their own methods, for applying mask work to the exploration of the elements. The exercises mentioned below are just an introduction to some of the many more that can be done. A whole book could be written on this topic.

Earth

Action

Work with the image of a tree withstanding the wind, rooted into the earth. Have one person play "the tree", and one act as the wind upon you. Person A should root their feet into the earth, arms held aloft in a wide expansive gesture representing the foliage in a large oak or elm tree. Partner B uses some combination of gesture and sound, without actually making contact, to blow through the tree branches. Blow gently or harshly, and partner A move in response to the force of B without moving your feet. Stay anchored. While the wind is moving through you in different directions, the real point of the exercise for person A is to ground their center into the earth – to make a base that, no matter what, could weather any of the blows from up top by anchoring your energy deep below your pelvis into the floor. Trade off.

Then, working as individuals, try the image of a clay sculptor, digging lumps of clay out of the earth, smacking them together, standing in wide second position, raise the lumps of clay together high over your head, and with a full body throw down into the earth, leading from the hips, throw the clay lump on the ground with a loud "splat", letting the fingers spread wide and end in a period facing the ground flat. Say "splat" as the clay lump hits the floor. Make sure the actions are strong and definite, with no bounce or "echo" in the action. The point is to further engage the body in actions that are solid and forceful, getting your hands dirty and your mind into a kind of strong, physical work. Earth imagery should lead to movements, language, and characters that have a low center of gravity and are "grounded", salt-of-the-earth types who say what they mean.

After doing these two exercises, move out into the space retaining the effect of earth imagery on your actions. Obviously, a rock, dirt, tree, stone doesn't really move. The part of the imagery that is valuable to an actor is the part that can move *while* maintaining an inner image of earth that colors your actions. Think about all the times you have met a "stony stare", someone whose demeanor was "hard as a rock", thought that someone's explanation was "muddy". There are many ways earth as an image can manifest. Spend at least 20 minutes within the element, doing group or solo explorations before moving on to the next one.

Variations

With each element, it is important to think of the scale of dynamics from the lowest end to the highest. At rest, we have a rock. On the higher end, we have earthquakes, volcanoes, and other events of cataclysmic power. Embody through side-coaching the full range of possibilities.

Air

Action

Fly around the room with your arms extended like an airplane. Feel the breeze going over the surface of your skin. Use your hands as paddles, keeping them parallel to the floor if you want to cut through space. To turn, rotate your left palm perpendicular to the floor, and use the imaginary air resistance to turn your body counterclockwise, as if you were going around a pole. Right-hand paddle turns your body clockwise. Both hands turned flat to the wind will stop you. Rotate palms to the floor again to start moving, and slice through space.

Variations

Once one person has warmed up the space and run as fast they could using their hands as guides, add another, then another, until you have five to six people running through the space at full speed, passing and weaving through each other's flight paths without colliding. It's an exhilarating feeling, and begins to transfer to the body some sense of what it is to be a molecule moving at the speed of the wind, with a sense of its power.

Then, imagine that everyone in the room represents a portion of the air in the space. Distribute evenly, so that any motion made by one "molecule" affects another. Choose one person to travel through the air, stirring things up, and seeing how one molecule hits another without actually colliding. Always allow a cushion of air around each body, and move until the natural energy delivered by the instigator disperses through the space. See if you can stir up a tornado, or hurricane, by getting all of the molecules spinning around the room in an organized fashion.

Convert all the wind/air imagery into speech. Try talking with "gusto" while moving through the space. Do the first couple of lines of Lear's speech to the storm, "Blow winds and crack your cheeks...". Do the low end too, carrying on a gentle conversation with someone, guided by the image that both of you are just "breezing" along. Air can go from still, dense, calm, or arid to bombastic tirades full of "hot air" or inspirational soaring rhetoric like the "I have a dream..." speech of Martin Luther King. Try all states.

Fire

Action
Sit in a circle on the floor with a group of six to ten people, backs to the center and bodies facing out. Close your eyes. Going from the smallest spark of an idea through the full life cycle of fire, start expressing in every way you can the image of fire. Be the smoke, be the sparks, be the flames licking upward, just begin bringing the idea of being on fire to life, not you as a person burning, so much as you as the spirit of fire growing from the smallest smoke and spark to a full-scale bonfire. If that means roaring up on your feet and jumping and leaping around the room, that is up to you. Open your eyes when you need to, and keep them open as the fire rages until you end up back down at the end to a pile of ashes and burned-out, smoking wood. Whatever "fuel" you are using to burn with, it is both an individual and a group exercise. You do not need to do exactly what everyone else does, but you should be aware of the energy of the group and those near you, so that your image blends with theirs. After the fire has "peaked", let it start to decay, until everyone stops moving, and the fire goes out.

Water

Action

The journey of water begins with the image of a small spring, born out of the rock at the top of a hill. The spring trickles down the slopes of a hill, gathering volume and growing into a brook, a rushing stream that spills into a large lake. Journey as a lake however you see fit, imagining that you are both wide and deep, with a sense of stillness and calm moving slowly towards the next transition: a waterfall, a high-energy freefall of water splashing and spilling over a dam and downstream into a large, wide, shallow gravely river that moves downhill until it meets the ocean. When you reach that vast end point, end the exercise and wait for everyone to get there.

Water has fabulous lessons to teach actors; it has so many properties, is so malleable, able to go from gas to liquid to solid. Speech can babble/bubble, or roar into action like a waterfall, but the beauty of water, even in its most destructive states, is that it does not carry tension. Energy, yes, tension, no.

For more advanced exercises, you can combine elements. Have a group of actors work on fire, and another group work on water. Bring the two groups together to negotiate an issue, add dialogue, and see how it transforms. Or take a journey through an imaginary natural terrain, walking along a beach, through a forest, up a hill, across a stream. Then have it impacted by changing elements. Water begins to boil, wind blows through the trees, a fire in the forest drives you to the river, which freezes, and so on.

Working the microsecond and the millimeter

Action

Work with a simple action: sitting in a chair, picking up a pencil, reaching for another person's hand. The nearer you get to completing the action, the more you can "put on the brakes". Don't freeze up or let your energy get rigid. Think of it as a hydraulic compression, adding density and commitment to the last phase of any action, slowing it down the most just as you reach your goal. The last few millimeters and microseconds are very important. I call it milking the moment. It should be explored with every part of your body. It will give new meaning and depth of emphasis to your actions. Eventually, a simple action like two people looking at each other and moving closer together can stir up tremendous imbalances and feelings of joy, panic, fear, hatred, and attraction. Learn to swim in the tensions, and not break them. Every impulse to move or react to another actor can be amplified to its maximum. Relish the millimeters and the microseconds as key tools your body can use for constant, present provocation.

Text and physicality

These next exercises focus on language and physicality. The voice is obviously an important part of the physical tools of an actor, and these improvisations help to develop energy levels, dynamic planes, and ensemble interaction through body and voice.

Dramatic planes of action

Every action on stage takes place on one of three planes, or a combination of them: the horizontal, the vertical, and the diagonal (oblique). Each plane is key to unlocking specific, universal dramatic terrains. The Laban system (see below) uses some of this vocabulary; the version I discuss here originated at the Lecoq school. These dramatic planes of action are worth exploring individually and experiencing vocally, physically, and psychologically. Doing so will make actors more present and connected to their own psycho-physical equipment. Once solo work is complete, it is also an excellent basis for group choral work. M. Lecoq employed these planes of action as one of several tools for approaching classical Greek chorus work.

Action

Take a 4–5-foot pole and use it to explore all the actions you can on one plane. The point is not to use the stick as a narrative object (spyglass, crutch, gun) but as a line of force that carries your focus and action out into the room in a specific way. Start with *horizontal* actions. Do everything you can, fast, slow, high, low, move the pole and follow it, reverse it, go in opposition to it, and open yourself to all events, and eventually words and actions, that the horizontal plane can give you. Use the pole to inform all parts of the body: chest on the horizontal, or hips on the horizontal, not just your head. Then get into a group of five to six. Pick a leader. Have everyone follow that person in a chorus, keeping the sticks moving in the same direction at the same time. Use sound. Go through the space. Stop and talk about what you notice on that plane. The *horizontal* plane is a direct, combative space, where all personal conflicts take place, all forward and backward movements occur, and large, energetic forces are unleashed.

Switch to the *diagonal.* Start solo again. Notice the change in psychology? The color of your actions is different, but still push yourself not to be mesmerized – explore the full range of dynamics while staying on the diagonal. When working the diagonal, do not let your focus drift back to the horizontal. Explore all possibilities. Add sound. Try it in a group and stay together. Discuss the differences. The *oblique* is a much more poetic space, with a sense of infinite and suspended horizons. No real conflict with others, and more of a shared sense of awe, wonder, fear, or hope, and perhaps sorrow on the downward diagonal. This is a melodramatic and spiritual plane.

End by going to the *vertical*: up or down. Things become quite extreme, it is the most terminal place to go – either heaven or hell. Feelings reach the extreme almost immediately. Play with compression, speed, opposition – focus up while moving down, or focus down while pulling up towards the peak. Give voice, notice what thoughts are provoked, what situations work on that plane. Despair, anguish, ecstasy, pain, death, powerlessness jumps to the front, awareness of others disappears. It is a very solitary and powerful plane. It is the ultimate tragic plane.

Go back to working with a leader in a group, and move intentionally between all three planes. Use the change in planes and dynamics to feed a group impulse. Follow along, and move throughout the whole space. Explore transitions from one plane to the next. Slow, sudden, deliberate. Get two or three groups going at the same time, let them interact and respond to each other's actions.

Variations

You can eventually remove the sticks, and work the groups with the same awareness and energy using just eyes, arms, and torsos. Take it back to solo work, and apply it to a monologue from Shakespeare. Find places in the text where the actions can move from one plane to the next while speaking the text. Map a whole sonnet based on how it moves in three dimensions through space.

Any action taken to the maximum can also be taken to the minimum. After working the whole space using sticks, try being stationary and take a one-minute journey through all three planes using just the eyes and the breath. Sustain the dramatic intensity you discovered, but internalize the movement.

Escalations: Scale of laughter

Action

This is a Lecoq exercise. Put six to seven people on a bench, side by side, starting in a completely neutral and relaxed state. The person on the end of the bench starts with the smallest increment up the scale of laughter – a twinkle in the eye, a pleasant thought – nothing too big. The pattern of this exercise is that the end person turns to the person next to them, who rises to that level and passes it on down the line, like the old kids' game of "telephone". People in the middle are responsible for matching the new state and maintaining it as they pass it on, and turn back out front facing the audience. When it reaches the end person, they take the state, face the audience, and bump it up a notch. Then they pass it back down the line the other way. The energy of the laugh continues to grow, with the two end people bumping it up, and the ones in the middle passing it on and sustaining it. As the state of laughter grows, the group will go from twinkle to smile to giggle to chuckle to laugh to full-scale guffaw, ending at dying-for-breath hysteria. As the group goes up the scale, the pattern usually breaks down, and anyone who thinks they can bump it higher should, and everyone has to match that new height of laughter.

After the peak, let it all settle back down gradually, till everyone catches their breath, and start over with a new group.

Variations

This works equally well with the Scale of Anger. Just watch out for injuring your voices or engaging in physical violence.

Another good exercise is to allow the group to develop a new scale once it reaches a peak. There is usually some kind of organic metamorphosis on the slide back down towards a new direction. Allow that to become a new scale, of fear, or confusion, or silliness, or whatever takes hold. In this way, the group can ride up and down several dynamic rollercoasters, while also training themselves to stay on the same theme, develop communication skills, surpass their personal limits, and so on.

Escalations: Scale of fear

Action

This is my own variation. It is an excellent ensemble exercise for developing awareness of others, and how much room you have at the top or bottom of a scale to take it further. Start with a group of five to seven. If you have five people, make it a scale with five steps. If you have seven, use seven steps. The lowest first step builds towards the top step, full-scale panic and hysteria. All actors go outside the room. The first person enters the room through the door, creating the first step up the scale of fear. Don't do too much. Person 1 may enter with just a slight feeling of unease, a state of alert as if they heard something. As each person enters, they take it up a notch, entering in a higher state of fear, affected by both their own imagination and the actions of the other people in the room. The next to last step should go to almost the highest point possible, and everyone in the room rises to each new level as more people enter. The last person in is the payoff to the whole scale: either the reason they are afraid, the resolution to what that fear buildup was for, the antagonist to all the previous people who entered and created the tension. Resolve it any way you can.

Escalations: States of pride

The next three exercises come from Lecoq. They help actors learn the difference between faking a reaction and really being stimulated into a genuine reaction to external forces.

Action

Three to four players are the "experimenters", with one person sitting in a chair center stage the subject. The chorus of players escalates the state of pride of the person at the center. Begin with non-verbal actions, then move to language as needed to raise the state of pride of the subject in the chair. Ask for their autograph, take group pictures, praise their abilities, and do what is needed to provoke a genuine escalation in the subject.

Variations

As the peak is being reached, have someone in the group change course. Finding a little chink in the armor, a discovery that the person you were praising is not so great or was someone else, or their response didn't please the group, leads to a whole new set of feelings: abandonment, ridicule, humiliation, desperation, all can be provoked by the group "turning" on you. *Do* be careful, and talk it out a bit afterwards. People can take this too personally if you aren't careful. Make sure everyone understands this is an exercise, anything goes in it, but try not to wound the actual actor. Yes, it feels great for everyone when their ego is being fulfilled and praised: telling someone they are actually fat or ugly in this framework is the wrong use of the exercise. Stay in the world of imagined circumstances.

Escalations: The wedding speaker

These next two exercises place the idea of escalation into a realistic social situation that can start in naturalism and escalate to the absurd. They are good structures for building controlled improvisational themes and invention.

Action

Set up a situation where one person is the best man or woman at a wedding, making a speech about the married couple (who are not present in the exercise). Everyone else is a wedding guest. Gradually escalate interruptions for the person speaking. While they are trying to speak, go up the scale of noises, sidebar comments, catcalls, and comments to unnerve the person speaking. As with any escalations, start small. Give them room to get started, but as the crowd "turns" on the speaker, and the dynamic in the room builds as a conflict grows, make it a linear escalation. It can't go down, it just goes higher/faster until the person trying to speak either breaks through and regains control of the room, or is completely derailed and gives up trying to talk.

Escalations: A funeral

Action

Do the same action at a funeral. Have one person decide what their relation is to the deceased, and have them start to speak at the service, when the rest of the room finds a way to begin to escalate some kind of interruption. It could be a giggle because of something that was said, that builds into a full-scale suppressed wave of laughter breaking out in counterpoint to the gravity of the speaker, or it can be a disagreement over the facts of what the person is saying that takes it into a full-scale, inappropriate debate over politics or family lore.

Gesture and text

This section offers a few systematic ways of approaching text. When do you use stylized movement? When do you turn a play on its head with a mash-up? When should you be as faithful as possible to the stage directions? Once you unlock a theatrical event from naturalism, the sky is the limit and the number of choices can be overwhelming. But there are a few basic patterns that appear in the work of most theater and dance companies that combine text and physicality. An awareness of these options can help you develop your own work (Figure 2.1).

On the simplest of levels, you have four main choices.

- Speak, and then move.
- Move, and then speak.
- Move and speak simultaneously.
- Move while other people are speaking (live or recorded).

When you create movement that supports or counterpoints a text, you are working with actions or gestures that fit somewhere on a scale from most realistic to most abstract. Variations include:

Naturalistic: Typical actions associated with human behavior (e.g., smoking a cigarette, waving hello, scratching an itch).

Mimetic: Illustrative gestures that suggest a specific action or object without the actual props (e.g., the cooking sequence in the opening scene of Thornton Wilder's *Our Town*).

Sensual: Gesture that evokes a quality or mood (e.g., ears flicking and tails twitching on the horses in *War Horse* to evoke nervousness, or movements triggered by a sensual response to pleasure or pain).

Figure 2.1: Samurai 7.0, *Beau Jest Moving Theatre (Lisa Tucker and Davis Robinson), Boston Center for the Arts, Boston, MA 2006. Photo: Justin Knight*

Symbolic: Metaphoric action that comments on the text (e.g., Laura playing with glass animals in *The Glass Menagerie*, people tearing pages out of a book while a eulogy is being read, Rhinoceros' running through a café in Ionesco's play *Rhinoceros*).

Expressionistic: Gesture rooted in an emotional reaction (e.g., the letter reading/writing sequence in the play *Black Watch*).

Contrapuntal: Gestures that run counter to what is being said (e.g., speaking calmly while gesturing wildly, or moving slowly and gracefully while text is in a frenzy).

Random: Gesture made with no connection to the text (e.g., choreograph phrases first, then add text afterwards with no effort to link the two).

Each of these gestures serves different dramatic purposes. As ensemble creators, you may have a strong feeling of what you want to say and how you want to say it, or you may need to try variations in order to decide what feels right. Look at the overall piece and at each individual scene to determine what gestures will most effectively express your ideas. Sometimes an action saves a thousand words; sometimes one phrase saves a thousand movements. Test your material out by pushing it in both directions, from most realistic to most abstract. Let your instincts be your guide, and reflect as a group on what best communicates your needs, your story. Bring in trusted outside eyes to watch and give you feedback. Here are some exercises that expand gestural range and clarity.

Physical monologues

Action

Pick a piece of text. Instead of a character saying what they are thinking and feeling with text, start by "moving" the ideas/feelings physically with no text for a minute or two. Try using a piece of music that feels right. Use your whole body, from your core to your extremities, and move "out loud", saying what has to be said using movement instead of text.

Committing to a gesture

Action

Make a spontaneous gesture or action that is repeatable. Milk it; look for what is at the source of the action by going faster or slower, louder or softer, until you find full satisfaction with what was at the root of that initial impulse. Throw it away, and start a new one. With each repetition, let the source of the impulse amplify the action, and the action amplify the feeling. Add sound. Find within three to four repetitions the full flowering of what that action wants to express. Any action or gesture, made with commitment, can be the kernel of an idea that deserves deeper exploration. This is a good way to expand people's range, encourage risk, and develop a habit of moving with purpose and commitment. It also helps make the psycho-physical connection apparent, so that all movement encourages an emotional connection, and any thought or impulse can find a physical outlet.

Variation

Do the same exercise, but create a gesture in response to a specific word, theme, or image (e.g., nostalgia, revolt, panic: words that trigger a response). Make an extended phrase that you can remember and repeat, play with all variations.

Expanding a gestural vocabulary

Some people will have a hard time breaking away from mimetic or naturalistic gesture because they haven't been exposed to alternatives. They have spent so much time moving a certain way that other choices don't come naturally. If they haven't seen much modern dance or non-naturalistic drama, they will have limited role models. To free people up, a simple exercise is to take an event and put it through all versions of gesture possible.

Action

Choose a simple event (e.g., eating dinner with your family, mowing the lawn, walking your brother to school). For text, have someone else read out loud any text you like related to the event for a template. In an actual performance, the actor who is moving may be speaking, but for this exercise, free the actor from speaking so they can focus on their gestural range.

- Act the event out naturalistically without dialogue.
- Find four to five mimetic gestures that capture the experience, and open the gesture patterns up to changes in perspective (visual vernacular), miniaturizing, shorthand, spelling things out, illustrating, or amplifying any actual moments that occur to you in creative ways.
- Essentialize the flow of the event without punctuating each action, and free the gestures up to evoke a broader, looser feeling of what happens. Let mood start to affect how fast or slow you go, when the tempo changes, when the actions get darker or lighter, heavier or breezier. "Dance" the whole event in 30 seconds physically.
- Zero in an emotional reaction to the event. Go through from beginning to end without illustrating any literal actions. Instead, express physically how it feels at each stage of the event to be in the situation or to be watching it from the sidelines. See if you can boil it all down to one psycho-physical action that expresses your reaction to the event, what Michael Chekhov calls a psychological gesture.
- Try an abstract gesture pattern that comments on the geometry of the event, the architecture of the event, the players in the event, the voice of the speaker, the pattern of shadows in the room.
- Do something contrapuntal. Choose two to three gestures that can be repeated that run counter to your emotional or literal experience of the event, that can be repeated while the event or text from the event is playing out in opposition to those gestures.
- Copy three to four gestures from someone else's piece and apply them to yours, so that their genesis has no relationship to your material, and see what affect random coincidence has on meaning.

None of these methods are sure-fire, magic bullets for creating good work, but they are all ways of expanding your tool set so that you have a richer expressive palette as an ensemble.

Non-naturalistic gesture

When an action happens on stage that evokes an emotional reaction, such as Juliet discovering Romeo dead, audiences recognize and empathize with the grief and anguish found in the loss of a lover. In naturalistic acting, audiences admire the actors who most convincingly play that scene on stage as if they really were the lovers, encouraging a willing suspension of disbelief. In the postmodern era much was done to deconstruct that pattern, creating a movement score before giving actors the text, or staging work in non-literal ways that allowed the audience to be aware they are in a theater with actors and see the event from a new perspective without strictly identifying with the actor's world of make-believe. Shows began to use space, music, language, symbolic design, abstract blocking, and other tools to challenge conventional modes of emotional identification and reception of story.

The experiments of the avant-garde theater movement paved the way for a renewed interest in story and emotion, albeit one using a more sophisticated range of tools. We are at a point culturally where complex actions and sophisticated narrative devices are being used by ensembles to tell stories that have an emotional impact on audiences, while still challenging accepted notions of traditional forms of drama. In some cases, we are moved and don't know why. In others, we are told two stories at once. Work has become increasingly mediated, with video screens, sound design, and abstract blocking creating several layers of meaning. The variety of great work being made now by established theaters and touring ensembles indicates that we have passed through a postmodern phase of challenging mainstream theater conventions, and entered a new theatrical era where ensembles around the world are exploring a theater that is part text and part visual, part movement and part musical. Often these tools are being applied to a growing field of work that is socially relevant, politically significant, or community-based, work that interrogates race, gender, class, and issues of social justice.

Audiences were deeply affected by the National Theatre of Scotland's *Black Watch*,[13] which returned to New York several times. This was true also for Kneehigh Theater's[14] production of *Brief Encounter* and Improbable Theater's[15] *Shockheaded Peter*. These shows came back to New York for repeat, sold-out showings. These productions are technically sophisticated in some places, and straightforward in others. They blend contemporary theatrical devices and old-fashioned stage savvy. New York-based devising ensembles like Big Dance Theater, The Elevator Repair Service, The Debate Society, and The Wooster Group all use non-naturalistic movement, video or audio, and dance phrases to reveal a *deeper* meaning in the material while still connecting to an audience on an emotional and narrative level. This, for me, is a very positive trend for the future of theater. The success of shows like *War Horse, 39 Steps, Gatz, Peter and the Starcatcher*, and *Brief Encounter* points towards an appetite in contemporary audiences for new directions in staging.

At the annual Theatre Communications Group(TCG) conference in 2011, ensemble devising was barely mentioned. At the conference in 2012, several panels and breakout sessions were heavily attended, and larger mainstream theaters are now teaming up with ensemble companies to create new works. The opening ceremonies at the 2012 Olympics in London were choreographed with thousands of volunteers who used simple, clear, direct gestures in an organized fashion to evoke images of pastoral England, the Industrial Revolution, childhood dreams and nightmares, and other broad themes that used gesture filled with emotional energy and non-mimetic narratives. When I began writing this book there were around 100 companies in the Network of Ensemble Theaters experimenting with original work. Now there are over 300, holding regional and national conferences every year. Groups like the M/B Adaptors developed a performance language they now teach to others at the Margolis Training Center[16], and more alternative training programs open up every year. There are companies around the world pushing the boundaries of expression with new media tools and new models for structure and collaboration that have yet to be seen.

Here are some basic exercises for unlocking actions from naturalism. I do these exercises with student actors doing ensemble work, and with my own company when developing new material.

Gesture Rounds

This is a variation on the Rounds exercise mentioned earlier in this chapter. It is similar in concept to Michael Chekhov's[17] idea of finding a psychological gesture. Do a simple action, repeat it, and see where it takes you. Invest in it. Let it grow intuitively. What is the full flowering of that gesture? What expresses that impulse best? Should it accelerate or slow down? Become more complex or simpler? And how does one person's action affect the next person's action?

Action

In its simplest form, a group of five to six people form a semicircle and leave a large area in front of them for the person "on stage" to do some gestural brainstorming. One person jumps up, faces the "audience", starts a gesture/action and explores it for about 15–30 seconds, then sits down and someone else jumps up and immediately follows their impulse (which can be directly affected by the previous person or not). People observe what is going on without planning or discussing, while staying ready to jump in next. People can go in any order – whoever has the strongest impulse goes. This version of Rounds is called Open Rounds.

Variations

You can do Rounds with more people (two people up at a time together) and Rounds on a *theme*. For example, if you were making a piece about museum guards, you can do a series of Rounds on that specific theme. Everyone jumps up and tries something prompted by that theme. *No* discussion or planning is needed, no excuses or explanations of what you were trying to express. Just go around several times and get impulses in front of the group doing mimetic, expressive, abstract, or chaotic actions that are somehow fed by your exploration of the world of museum guards. It might be triggered by the paintings themselves, guard behavior, expressions of boredom or panic; whatever comes up. You can grab another person or two if the image or action you have an impulse to explore needs more bodies: just quickly whisper to them as you are standing up and tell them what you need them to do.

You can continue this work on Group Rounds on a Theme by adding language. People can test out snippets of dialogue or language triggered by the theme. It is also very useful to do rounds on a theme with added limitations as you explore more deeply: try the same prompt but with no use of hands or arms, all dialogue and no movement, add props, or do monologues or gestures with a specific time limit (e.g., only five seconds, go for two minutes, and so on).

Experiments with text

Here is an example of how my ensemble approached a specific piece of text. In our production of *Motion Sickness*, we spent two weeks determining how to physicalize the dictionary definition of nausea. We put the definition on an index card, and played with different ways of reading/speaking/dancing the text. After several tries we settled on an "outside" voice, the show's pseudo-guide/narrator, speaking the text to the audience while walking naturalistically on stage. As he did so, the other characters in the show came on stage in tableaus and went through individual movement patterns of expressionistic gestures of their own journey in the play, while the narrator walked around them like a museum exhibit. This built up to a mimetic choral group vomit matching a vocal escalation by the guide that led to a running sequence contrapuntal to what was just said.

Our particular choices aren't important, but the method we used to arrive at our choices can apply to any project. Trial and error using the list of options below will help you arrive at what works. Use reflection and discussion after rehearsal to check your intuition against the spine of the story. Is there enough Joy, Skill, Risk, Momentum, or Surprise in the work? Do the discoveries lead to a physicalization of the text you love or hate?

Action
Take a piece of text important to your show. Start with a short sample, be it from a novel, an interview, something composed, or a

piece of dialogue. Print it out or memorize it. Then experiment with the four main possibilities.

- Move first then pause and speak, using short sections of the text followed by more movement and text, or as one whole phrase of text after movement.
- Speak the text first, then move.
- Try speaking and moving at the same time.
- Have someone speak the text while others move. That someone can be a recording, a live actor, or, as is common these days, a media projection of spoken or printed text. You can also use the technique of speaking into a microphone, which has the effect of creating the feeling of inner thoughts being spoken.

The first few times, let actors do what comes intuitively for gestures/actions. After a few tries you will see which of the four main methods seems the most promising. Let's say it's the fourth version. Next, take that version and push the gestures through the scale, from naturalistic to random, from pianissimo to frenzied. See whether imagistic, contrapuntal, or naturalistic gesture has the desired impact. Step back and look at the whole piece, and determine whether at this point in the show it is more important to draw attention to an intellectual concept, create a poetic effect, or cause an emotional reaction. These are the questions you need to ask throughout the development of a piece that will inform your choices for using Text and Physicality.

Variation

A completely different approach that produces interesting counterpoint is to take the same page of text, and change the settings. Pick four different locations (e.g., a subway, an airplane, a forest, and an office). See how the text plays out while doing everyday actions associated with that location. This was an exercise I heard about from the Elevator Repair Service,[18] and makes for very interesting work. The clarity of the setting often illuminates different aspects of the text. This is a good exercise for ungluing people from naturalistic acting, while still maintaining a sense of meaning and connection to what is being said.

Scene-study exercise

Action

Choose a scene for two to three actors from a classic play such as *The Importance of Being Earnest*, *Who's Afraid of Virginia Woolf*, or *The Children's Hour*. Learn a page of the text. Mark it through one time making the realistic blocking choices that actors would typically make. Now throw that away, but do not throw away the search for *meaning connected to feeling.* Pick an interesting place to start physically, and don't be afraid to use the floor, objects, weight engagement, and any other start point that is not literal. Feel the rhythm of the words, or their muscularity. Work out a movement pattern a sentence or two at a time that expresses something you can connect to while saying those lines. Just don't spell out what you are saying. When the text is saying 2+2, you don't need to say 4. What happens if you speak while leaning against each other and rise up slowly back to back? What happens if one of you is on the floor and the other is sitting on them? Notice the impact these non-naturalistic choices have on observers, and how a new story is generated. What happens if you choreograph a two-minute movement sequence and then put the text on top of the action? Do interesting coincidences provide another layer of meaning to the text?

Pursue those pathways that your instincts and the audience's reactions tell you are richest. Some texts may take quite a bit of working out without any speaking at first, then put the text back in. Pause where needed. Try to make the movement story flow as one event, just as the text does. In short order, you will have another way of telling the story that brings new meaning to a play, and which can take into account current thinking on race, class, gender, and politics in a way that may make a dated problematic play relevant again, or introduce an old chestnut of a play to a new generation raised on YouTube, MTV, cell phones, and other influences of the 21st century that weren't a part of the culture when the play was written.

Variation

Take one line of text in a play, and with two to three actors, try three different approaches to staging the same line of text as if it were the beginning of a show. Invert, echo, or move the text between the actors in a way that releases the energy of the words without feeling like one person has to play Iago and another plays Othello. Present all three together as one piece. I like to create choices using the weight and gesture exercises mentioned earlier, and play off of some of the implied psychological subtext in the play or find moments that aren't in the text but could be part of the character's world.

Formal movement systems

Laban

Rudolf Laban developed a comprehensive system for analyzing and describing movement that is organized by Body, Effort, Shape, and Space. This system is very thorough, and used by many dancers and movement theater practitioners. It requires years of training to fully master, and is well explained elsewhere, so it is not gone into here. Certified Laban practitioners can be found throughout the United States. It *is* a very useful and practical methodology that can provide ensembles with a common physical vocabulary and a way of creating and analyzing material. It is taught at colleges and universities, and workshops can be found in the practice worldwide. See http://www. limsonline.org/ for more information.

The *Alexander Technique* is a system of movement analysis developed by F.M. Alexander, also with a worldwide network of formal training to become a certified teacher of the method. It is commonly used by actors and singers to correct alignment problems and develop a freer and more effective way of moving and speaking. Many colleges and universities employ trained Alexander teachers to work with their students. It is less of an ensemble movement vocabulary, and more a system that requires individual one-on-one lessons. See http://www.alexandertechnique.com/ for more information.

Viewpoints

One of the biggest developments in training recently has been the growth of interest in Viewpoints. This is a movement-based system that uses several modern dance concepts codified by dancer Mary Overlie, and further refined by the directors Ann Bogart and Tina Landau. Viewpoints help actors develop an awareness of themselves and their relationship to space, time, and others. It is the primary tool, along with Suzuki training (not the violin method), of the SITI Company in their devising work. Directors often use Viewpoints as a way to help organize bodies on stage. There are regular workshops in Viewpoints, and well-written books explaining the methods, so there is no need to go into them here. Both "founders" have websites with information on training, with either Mary Overlie (http:// sixviewpoints.com/index.html) or Ann Bogart and the SITI Company (http://www.siti.org/trainingschedule.htm). The SITI Company is also the main source for training in Tadashi Suzuki's methods in the United States. The actress Ellen Lauren, who works with SITI, is one of the few Americans to have studied directly with Mr. Suzuki and who has his permission to teach his methods in the United States.

Learning to work with any of these movement systems will not, per se, result in a well-written show. They are tools, and need to be applied with passion and rigor to subject matter that engages the ensemble. They are not themselves performance forms. They are training methods, diagnostic systems, and philosophies of movement that help to teach actors a way of moving and thinking.

Contact Improvisation

Contact Improvisation is a dance form developed by Steven Paxton and others.[19] It is a tool I find very useful for learning how to share weight, how to communicate without dialogue, and how to see opportunities while working with a partner. When it first swept campuses in the 1970s, people would put on improvised contact jams as public performances. I lived in Amherst, Massachusetts, where many of the founders lived and taught, so the area was inundated with contact jams for several years. I noticed that while the dancers enjoyed themselves thoroughly and were often quite skilled, audiences were less enthused. The lack of dynamics, the similar look of the work over time, led to mildly engaging shows that soon became more of a social dance form than a public event.

It is wonderfully energizing for participants to learn new techniques like Contact Improvisation or Viewpoints or Laban terminology in a workshop, but it is usually less interesting to watch that training presented on stage as if it were a final performance. Contact Improvisation is a valuable method for dealing with weight exchange and flow, and the field has grown into a very useful rehearsal tool. Its value as a performance form has faded, but its technical use in contemporary dance is now widespread. Take a look at how contact is used in the stunning work of dancers like Bridgeman/Packer[20] and Tere O'Connor.[21] Workshops on Contact Improvisation are now held worldwide.

Ensemble devising requires both sides of the brain, the analytical left and the chaotic and intuitive right. It's just my opinion, but I think that Viewpoints, Laban work, the Alexander Technique, and other formal, orderly systems need to be used in tandem with practices that encourage debate, disorder, and conflict. I say dirty it up a little. The orderliness of any formal system helps actors achieve clarity and efficiency, but meaning requires a healthy dose of the messier, more passionate side of creativity. Introduce some doubt, conflict, and "messy" humanity into the work to capture a true reflection of the human condition on stage.

We've gone from simple awareness exercises, walks, and weight exchanges to complex ideas of gesture and meaning in this chapter. Now it is time to apply those skills to making work. The next chapter assumes you are ready to make pieces, which I call Short Prompts.

3 *Short Prompts*

This chapter begins the dramaturgical work of devising. These short prompts are ways of getting at aesthetic issues and choices – what is this piece about? Why perform these actions in this particular order? Would it work better this way? What story are we telling? What story do we definitely not want to tell? What excites us? What moves us? What feels like a dead end? How do we resolve our disagreements over a piece?

This first exercise and its variations are a great way to start ensemble devising.

Lists

Action

Make a list of actions. Include contrasting elements. Work with a group of five to six actors to create a piece based on doing everything on the list. Present the piece.

This can be done in class or rehearsal and presented after a short rehearsal time limit (45 minutes works well). Lists also work well for creating longer, more complex pieces. Take a couple of days to rehearse before presenting the piece. After the first presentation, observers give feedback; what was startling, what worked well, what seemed to go on too long, what would they like to see more of? Actors then go off for a second round of development using those suggestions and any new ideas, and present it the next day. Two to three rounds of development can make for some really interesting pieces. No matter how complicated or obtuse the piece, the feedback process is always the same. Talk first about the things that worked, the most interesting moments. Then make suggestions for possible additions, deletions, or changes that the group can embrace or ignore.

A typical list for a beginning ensemble project might look like this.

Ensemble movement project

Include all of these actions in some form:

- three forward rolls;
- two shoulder rolls, forward or backward;
- one group tableau;
- a kiss;
- a slap;
- two log rolls;
- some running;
- a pause that is too long;
- a moment of aching beauty;
- a jump;
- a surprising entrance;
- something in unison;
- someone laughing or crying;
- three weight exchanges (lifts, leans, counterbalance);
- something symmetrical;
- something frightening;
- text from one newspaper article;
- groups of five to six actors;
- you may use music if you like;
- not everyone need do every action;
- do them in any order you like, repeat or add anything you need to;
- every moment should be fully committed, planned, and rehearsed;
- it need not make sense.

The beauty of working from a list is it gives the group a concrete starting point with achievable goals. It gets things started on a physical footing. It puts time pressure on the group so that the tendency to sit around and talk without working is circumvented. By starting with the physical, actors are encouraged to use their intuitive senses rather than analytically arguing over what to do and how their piece should be written. It is a much more right-brained process.

If you ask a group to write an original piece in an hour, they will usually start with questions like: What should this piece be about? Who are the characters? What will they say? What are their relationships? What is the conflict? The tendency to go right to plot and dialogue is universal. By just jumping in and doing actions on a list, other interesting and specific questions emerge: How long should we do this? When do we pause? Should we try that in unison? What if our moment of surprise happens here? What is a moment of aching beauty? How long is too long a pause? On occasion I have seen a group agree on a theme or thesis for a piece and plan it out before starting the physical work, but that tends to be the exception rather than the rule.

After a few awkward minutes, things start to percolate and great ideas are put on the table. A group aesthetic develops as the piece takes shape. Someone checks the list to see if anything is missing. A last minute run-through preps the group for their "showing". By focusing on solving the challenges on the list, the actors have unconsciously learned to work together, to use multiple levels, to think in a non-linear fashion, to tap their instinctual side, to share personal space and weight, and to develop a true spirit of ensemble cooperation. It's also a hell of a lot of fun to perform the pieces. In one exercise, an ensemble is born. If you are teaching devising or physical theater, this is a great starter exercise. Complete strangers can work together fluidly and come out best friends by the end of the day. Vastly different experience levels can be accommodated in one group. You can change the elements on the list periodically, but I have never failed to see interesting work made using these same or similar ingredients. Some groups are clumsy, some create a clear narrative with a beginning, middle, and end, some are graceful, some are wildly dangerous and chaotic. Keep a limit on the dialogue so that everyone engages with a physical commitment before thinking too much about text or meaning. I do think it is important to start out early with a little bit of dialogue and add in more complex text with succeeding exercises, but first make sure you have a group that has built a shared language physically. It's easier to work with complex text that incorporates a richer physicality by moving a lot first and then layering in language.

Variations

You can also make much shorter lists using only three to four elements, and devise projects that work well for duos and trios. The list above includes elements that are suited to larger groups. Some simple additions or deletions of the list can be done to solve smaller tasks or specific problems in the early stages of developing a new piece. Let's say you are part of a trio working on a piece about Dracula. The list might be:

- an opening image;
- a surprising entrance;
- two lines of dialogue that have to be said;
- a gesture repeated three times;

Or you may just focus on the moment of biting someone's neck:

- In pairs, find three possible gestures/images for neck biting.
- Use text from the Bram Stoker novel.

- Use text from Anne Rice.
- Physicalize internally one mood or image from a Bela Lugosi movie.
- Use Webster's dictionary.
- Move the text between you.

At the Lecoq school, lists are often used to develop material within a certain theatrical style. For instance, when exploring Melodrama, the prompt to a group would be to combine these elements in any order:

- a family;
- a betrayal;
- someone returning from war;
- there is a letter;
- a slap;
- a sudden entrance or exit.

Obviously, the ingredients of the list can push the piece in one direction or another, so choose elements that are important to the kind of work you want to make. Recently, three elements I am very interested in pursuing with students and with my company have been:

- the use of foreground and background on stage, as in a painting; finding contrasting or complementary images on different planes at the same time that exploit depth of field in the playing space;
- visual and emotional antithesis; bumping moments of bitterness up against something sweet: greed–generosity, tenderness–cruelty, pain and joy;
- using gesture in a non-literal way to layer the story being told, expressing images or thoughts in movement at the same time the text illuminates something else.

You can also make lists to guide the entire creation of a work, returning to it over a period of months. I heard that the genesis of the now-defunct Minneapolis-based company Theatre de la Jeune Lune's hit show *Yang Zen Frogs* began with a very short, simple prompt:

- Let's use everything stored in our studio from all previous shows.
- Let's evoke laughter at least once every 60 seconds.

That may just be a rumor, but it is an interesting prompt.

You can turn a list into a sentence, or a brief paragraph, and before you know it you have a mission statement. Some groups believe you can't begin a piece until you all agree on the goals, that the work begins with a manifesto or a mission statement. Like a business plan, this gives the group a vision to pursue and a thesis to defend when arguments develop over what does or does not belong in the piece.

I have certainly found in my own work with Beau Jest that the clearer and more heartfelt the premise of the piece, the better the product. We make our worst work when we start with a general idea, try to whittle it down, and convince ourselves the footing is solid when deep down inside we know it really isn't so. We built a house with no foundation. Ah well, you also learn from your mistakes...

Ugly/beautiful/ordinary/extraordinary

I learned this very useful short prompt in graduate school in a choreography class with Judith Chaffee at Boston University. First, we were assigned a short list – make a dance for three people, using one prop and one song. These were initially short etudes, made up over a weekend and presented during the next class, with everyone in trios learning each other's dances in a short amount of time.

Action
The next stage of development was to take that dance and do four things with it: make a moment that is beautiful, a moment that is ugly, a phrase that is ordinary, and a phrase that is extraordinary. This was a very liberating assignment. Suddenly we had been given permission to make the ugliest phrase possible, to aspire to something beautiful, to do something ordinary and something extraordinary. Dances were then presented again for feedback, and inevitably people had wildly differing reactions. Something one person found ugly, another person thought was extraordinary. The thing one person made to be beautiful seemed ordinary to someone else. This opened up everyone's thinking about their own taste and interests, and led to great aesthetic discussions.

Variations
I have found this prompt useful for almost any piece at any stage of development, and have combined it with many of the other ensemble-building exercises mentioned in this book. For instance, if you take a longer prompt, like doing a Shakespeare play in ten minutes or *adapting a paragraph* from a novel, first, present the original draft of the piece to the group. Then apply this list to it, and add in moments that are intentionally *ordinary*, *extraordinary*, *ugly*, and *beautiful*. Present again.

Joy/skill/risk/momentum

This is another useful set of guideposts I first heard about from the American clown Avner the Eccentric, which I believe originated with Carlo Mazzone-Clementi at the Dell'Arte[1] school of physical theater. Any successful piece of theater, scripted or not, usually always has these four elements.

As you are working on material, ask yourselves – is it lacking in joy? Do we need more momentum? What risks are we taking? Can we refine a moment with more skill? And by risk, of course I mean many things beside physical degree of difficulty. It might mean risking a moment of real intimacy, going into a relationship more deeply, or scratching below the surface to discover more vibrant and vulnerable acting values. Joy can be finding the pleasure in playing Richard III doing horrible things: it need not be about being "happy". Skill can be technical, as in singing in three-part harmony, or it can just be the way you shape an entrance or exit with care to the timing, momentum, and the careful set-up of the moments before. And momentum is a good word to think about when you present a piece and find the audience loses interest in it at a certain point. What can be done to sustain the momentum? What tempo shift/missing moment/pace variation/depth of commitment is needed to give the piece more momentum?

Action
After rehearsing any scene, ask yourselves whether it feels incomplete. If so, which of these four guideposts seems lacking: *Joy*? *Skill*? *Risk*? Or *Momentum*? Focus your next rehearsal on fixing that.

Titles

This is a structure that can be used with small or large groups. The title is often ambiguous or open-ended, in order to achieve the widest array of interpretations. Like a list, it sends the group down a certain path of inquiry with plenty of room for interpretation. I usually give groups an hour or so to work on a first draft, then present to the larger group. You can also do solos with titles.

Action
Give groups of two to three actors a title to work with. For small groups, I use titles like:

- A Slight Misunderstanding;
- Who Was That?;
- Too Much Information;
- The Nightmare;
- Every Second Counts;
- They Are Back.

Variations
It is also helpful to do Title work with assigned structures so that people intentionally explore different ways of problem-solving. Pick a title, and then use an assigned structure for how to approach it, such as:

- Rotating directors (each actor handles one part of the piece).
- Yes and . . . (everyone does every suggestion with no vetoes).
- Outside eye (one person sits out and shapes it all).
- Consensus (every choice is debated and chosen as a group).

You can combine the Title with physical tasks (use counterbalance twice, try disembodied voices at one point, change the rhythm four times, etc.) or solve the title with a predetermined aesthetic challenge (start with a manifesto, use depth of field, combine two contrasting elements). Any of these variations can be done using the same title, so that groups can then have a discussion about which tools, structures, or aesthetic challenges were the most satisfying or difficult to work with. Rotating decision-making models also helps people decide how they personally like to work, and gives them a few different approaches to use when stymied by a devising problem.

In an ensemble-devising workshop I co-taught at the Celebration Barn Theater[2] with David Gaines (an actor from the Moving Picture Mime Show and instructor at Lecoq's school), we used titles with small variations so that people could test out methods over the week to find their own best practice. Here are a few of the assignments from that week that explored Title/List/Structure variations.

Assignment

- Title: A Slight Misunderstanding.
- Size: Duets.
- Method: Equal among equals (Yes, and . . .).
- Tools: Your choice of text and movement.

- Title: Chosen by group-speak in unison (a Keith Johnstone exercise).
- Size: Trios.
- Method: Continue Yes, and . . . as a group.
- Tools: Narrative passed between members somehow: move the voice around.

- Title: Open improvisation, no theme.
- Size: Six people.
- Method: Start in duets, change partners, evolve to all six engaged; solo when needed.
- Tools: Counterbalancing, rhythmic work, and unison movement/pauses.

- Title: Frankenstein.
- Size: Duets.
- Method: Use three items on "the list" – your choice.
- Tools: Use some objects.

- Title: Continue with Frankenstein.
- Size: Duets.

- Method: Create a new beginning and a new ending.
- Tools: Have a third person watch and direct from outside.

- Title: Classic theme (Three Sisters, Hamlet, etc.).
- Size: Trio.
- Method: Develop a manifesto before you begin working.
- Tools: Use any tool we have used so far.

- Title: Family holidays.
- Size: Trios.
- Method: Democracy.
- Tools: Each actor offers one idea, group tries every idea.

- Title: Nightmare.
- Size: Trios.
- Method: Controlled democracy.
- Tools: Each actor offers one idea, group picks one to pursue at each juncture.

- Title: The Nightmare.
- Size: Trios.
- Method: Rotating directors.
- Tools: Each actor directs the piece for 15 minutes.

Lecoq was a master at using Titles and Themes with larger groups. Done as an auto cours (self-directed "homework") at his school in Paris, he would often send a group of nine students who spoke five different languages off into a corner of the studio to work for two hours on a piece called "In The Beginning" or "A Chance Encounter" and see what they came up with. I think he enjoyed watching people from around the world struggle to understand each other with these open-ended exercises that forced us to agree on what it was we wanted to do on stage to serve the theme. The only rule besides the title might be that there is one speaker, or there is a musician, or you must use the buffoon or neutral mask in creating this piece.

While there is real value to large group work, it can also be very frustrating. Louder voices tend to drown out quieter actors, and getting nine people to agree on anything is quite a chore. Do both. It is easier to use titles with smaller groups, and excellent work can be made using small variations on the tools, methods, or lists applied to the title. But the volume and power of a large group, when harnessed, can be exhilarating. It can open up new territory for actors and create exciting new narrative forms that are the basis for short or full-length works. At some point in devising you will come face to face with some very unpleasant disagreements. It is probably through that experience that you will also find out what kind of people you like to work with. This information is valuable for forming future ensembles.

Opening number

Action

An energizing short project from a Title is to get into groups of five to six and create an Opening Number to a show. This can range from emulating standard musical theater forms with dance choreography, singing, and acting; or it can be a dramatic opening sequence to a theatrical event that fully uses the dynamic talents of the people involved to imagine something three to five minutes long that propels the audience into the world of a new piece that hasn't yet been written. Choose a theme, and get to work. You should be able to do this in 45–60 minutes and then present it. It can use live music or recordings, spoken word or silence. Be specific about the "world of the play", and see what you can do to surprise/delight/horrify or engage an audience.

Variations

Chris Bayes, a theater teacher and director at Yale, does a fun version of this with an even shorter time span in his clowning classes.
In groups of four to five, students make up a song about someone in the class who is not in their group. The few rules are (another list):

- The song must be positive.
- Each member of the group has a solo.
- There must be a chorus.
- There must be choreography.

Rehearse for eight minutes, and then present. Once you do this, it is only fair to make up a number for every person in class, so do a few of these at the start of a session, until you have gotten around to everyone.

Word sculptures

Action

In groups of five to six, have someone outside the group call out an image. Actors keep their eyes closed for ten seconds to picture the image, then open their eyes and move into a three-dimensional sculpture of the word on a count of three, using each other to make one dynamic shape, not individual shapes, that expresses the Title. Hold the shape for a beat then extend it even further, to make it more fully that image. Viola Spolin has several exercises in this category in her classic book, *Improvisation for the Theater*. I learned these structures from Tony Montanaro at the Celebration Barn.
    Start with simple, open-ended words that have a sensual feel:

- red;
- orange;

- yellow;
- black.

Move on to more emotional/psychological shape sculptures, like:

- escape;
- betrayal;
- revenge;
- justice.

Think like a group making a new Henry Moore sculpture, or a Rodin installation.

Then try images with multiple layers, like:

- civil war;
- WWI;
- *Alice in Wonderland*;
- hell;
- the future;
- Gothic cathedral.

This is good preparation for seeing the body as a fully expressive, three-dimensional instrument.

Variations
Any one of these images can be planned and rehearsed. For instance, spend five minutes creating one image from *Alice in Wonderland* (i.e., the caterpillar smoking on the mushroom, Alice falling down the hole). Present them, notice variations, move on. Several images can be combined to create a short collage. This leads right into the Larger Prompt in the next chapter, Epic Tales in Short Times.

Paintings

Action
A very effective prompt for developing material is working from a painting. Put together a folder full of paintings/posters with a wide range of images and styles, from impressionistic works to modern art to traditional paintings by known masters. Get into groups of three to four actors. Lay out all the paintings on the floor, and browse them. Decide on one image as a group you want to work from. Make a one- to two-minute movement piece inspired by the painting. Don't worry about telling a story, or trying to reproduce the image. Play very loosely with the mood of the painting, the lines and brush strokes in the painting, the dynamic of contrasting colors, the detail in a corner or in the background. I think it is a good idea not to be too specific about what the finished "piece" should be like. Two groups may pick the same painting and come up with two radically different pieces, which is fine. It is also really useful to add music to the pieces.

Variations

Having a painting or central image is a very useful point of departure for the design time on any devised project. If the work is rooted in a specific aesthetic, find an image or painting to share with all of the designers and actors. This will guide everything from movement qualities and music composition to the costume designs and color palette of the set.

Work with a painting can also be done in a museum if you can get permission from a gallery where there is floor space to move around in front of the paintings. Some museum visitors may find it interesting to watch the results. And it can also evolve from a short prompt into something much larger and more involved. When the dancer/choreographer Martha Clarke[3] left Pilobolus to do her own work, the first major piece she built was a full-length work based on *The Garden of Earthly Delights* by Hieronymus Bosch. You can see examples of it on-line and begin to get an idea of how far this work can go. Another famous example of work inspired by a painting was the Stephen Sondheim/James Lapine piece about the painter George Seurat in *Sunday in the Park With George.*

Props and objects

When building a new piece, one often finds there is an object involved in the telling; some prop, some piece of fabric, something that helps define and communicate the story you want to tell. I have found it useful to have potential objects around the rehearsal hall early in the process, to develop ideas that couldn't be foreseen without the objects present, and to discover multiple uses. If you are working with designers, it also helps to boil down the world you are creating to one or two essential elements. Clarifying the objects will help inform the design. Here is a list of the objects we *had to* have early in rehearsal in some of Beau Jest's shows:

- *Ubu Roi*: Potatoes, burlap, and wooden poles;
- *A Mall and Some Visitors*: Plastic whirly pipes;
- *Motion Sickness*: Five chairs and a screwdriver;
- *Krazy Kat*: Bricks of all kinds;
- *War of the Worlds*: Death ray lamps and Foley sound effects;
- *Samurai 7.0*: Bamboo poles, toy horses, and grass fronds;
- *Ten Blocks on the Camino Real*: Skeletons;
- *Apt 4D*: A bench.

With other groups I have worked with (Figure 3.1):

- *The Fabulous Problemas*: A strong table and three chairs;
- *Moment of Impact*: A wooden toy train set and a trapeze.

Figure 3.1: Ten Blocks on the Camino Real, *Beau Jest Moving Theatre (Lauren Hallal, Lisa Tucker, and Robin Smith, puppet by Libby Marcus), Charlestown Working Theatre, Charlestown, MA, 2012. Photo: Jordan Harrison*

These objects work as their own kind of prompt, sometimes helping literally to advance the plot, or metaphorically changing the nature of the story from literal to poetic. In *The Fabulous Problemas*, a Colombian American clown trio that met at the Celebration Barn, it was determined early on that the setting was a café table in a foreign country. Once it was determined that the table needed to be weight-bearing, a table was built that also became a car, a bank vault, a map, a hide-out, a café, and the base for the finale of a complex physical stunt. In *Moment of Impact* (a solo show by Bronwyn Sims and the Strong Coffee Theater), the narrative involved the story of a train ride to a rehearsal of *The Master Builder* at Yale Repertory Theater that was interrupted by a suicide en route. One given was that the performer was interested from the beginning in combining narrative with aerial work and a trapeze of some kind. The addition of a wooden train set in rehearsal made possible transitions in the story-telling to several scales, and to a visual medium that allowed for a poetic moment best said through action, not words. The idea for using model trains and wood blocks was around for quite a while, but until they showed up in rehearsal none of their possibilities were apparent. Eventually, a set designer looking at an early draft of the show saw the image of the train tracks as something that could be continued up the wall and into the rigging, so the trapeze became a hanging ladder that allowed for aerial work.

Action

As you choose your theme or project, think about what objects or materials might help advance/create the world. Get them made, bought, built, found, and get them into the rehearsal room early on. Spend a few nights exploring what you do with them. Try it with music, with text, with a range of contact points within the narrative. See if you need to tweak or fine-tune the materials, the scale of them, or rig them to do something specific. And when you do find what you need, make or purchase back-ups, so that if it is lost or broken, it can be replaced. These days, products often come and go and you may never find the exact same object again.

Get several of the objects you have a hunch might be part of your piece. Let's say you think it's plastic water bottles. If you have an ensemble of five actors, I would start out by getting ten liter-sized bottles that are identical, a few smaller bottles, and several large plastic bottles. Empty some of them, and leave water in some. Introduce the objects to the ensemble, and give them a half hour or so to move with them, get used to their weight, see what different actions come to mind with no specific task assigned other than to just brainstorm for images, sounds, or movement patterns. Play some appropriate music at the same time for stimulation.

Variations

Start getting specific. Go through the story or theme you are developing, and see whether anyone has an idea for where the bottles can move the story forward. Is it a train image? An architectural image? Is there an image from nature like a storm, or wind blowing, or waves and the ocean? Send people off in pairs or solos to try to find solutions. After a few minutes, get back together and share what you have found. Often, the germ of an idea will present itself. It isn't long before that germ becomes a production number, or an essential part of the piece you are making. And it has been my experience that once you have something in the studio, it will get used again, often when you least expect it. Put the objects on a shelf nearby so that when you are further along with developing your piece, they are always right there for a moment of inspiration.

Moments of cruelty

Action

In groups of three or four, create a short scenario in which something very cruel is done to someone in the group. This is an exercise for getting people to find joy in unleashing their dark sides, something people often hold back on. It helps a group get specific, and figure out what is the difference between being mean, angry, or just plain cruel? How do they work together to evoke an emotional response in the audience? The most successful group is the one in which everyone watching says afterwards, "Now that was cruel!" It is a necessary step for being able to play vigorously and with a real impact on each other. When it is done right, you know it. Other people watching often have a visceral reaction to the scene. And the victim(s) in the group play an equal role in making the scene a success. It is a very specific action to focus group energies on.

Variations
Following the first round of presentations, if it doesn't elicit a real response, ask the group what would make it crueler? What about the set-up or the aftermath that is needed to make it stronger? Can silence be used more effectively? Does the moment of "attack" require more vocal color, more surprise, a better use of language? Is the real pathos in the scene during the action, or in the silence of the reaction afterwards?

I have also followed this exercise with Moments of Kindness, to provide some kind of balance after a couple of hours of working on being cruel, but inevitably those scenes were never as interesting.

Dropping bombs

Related to cruelty is the idea of anyone in a situation "dropping a bomb": saying or doing something that upsets the equilibrium of a situation. As a theme, bombs are a very useful way of looking at any surprising event on stage, from pleasant to macabre to absurd to infuriating. They show up in any performance that has a surprise. Two factors are in play.

● Every bomb (firecracker, grenade, landmine, tank shell, atomic) requires a corresponding crater the size of the explosion to ring true.
● The form of the crater/aftermath in any social group can involve all levels of awareness, from the people who notice it first and are most affected by it, to the people who notice it later and have less of a connection to it, to those who are oblivious that something momentous just happened.

Action
Start with a group of 10 to 12 people. Pick a setting where you would find a group (e.g., family gathering, high school reunion, the workplace, a lecture hall, a wedding, a funeral, etc.). Begin a realistic improvisation around that event to establish a couple of minutes of "normal" and believable behavior. Once a status quo has been

established, and relationships developed, anyone can be the one who "drops a bomb". Don't decide ahead of time what it is or who will cause it. Something always comes up. The main challenge is to not have more than one at the same time. When an event catches the group's attention, let it play out, complete with any action, entrances, role-playing, exits as needed, and allow a minute of aftermath for things to settle out with the group. Then start over, picking a new situation or theme. Notice the difference each time: how the dynamics of the bomb-dropping can change, and how the "crater" size afterwards must vary appropriately. Because it is an unplanned, spontaneous event, reactions tend to be genuine, a good thing to remember when staging a show with scripted lines in which surprises come along but too often are telegraphed or played predictably with no sense of surprise or impact.

Variations

Do the same set-up, but decide ahead of time which person is responsible for dropping a bomb, and let them pick the right time and place to do it. Repeat with a different person each time, so that everyone gets the experience of leading an event, or of reacting to one.

In groups of three to five, prepare a scene in which a bomb is dropped. The bomb can be verbal, an action, an emotional shock, a sudden reversal of events. Do just enough of a set-up to create the situation before the bomb, do the bomb, and then work on how the "crater" manifests itself afterwards. Play it through the reaction until the dust settles or a new direction starts. Best reaction wins.

You can also intentionally decide to practice differing scales of surprises. Start with a firecracker (a caustic remark, an overheard comment, a little joke or jab, a flash of the eyes or a smile that surprises), and then escalate in five to six steps up to bigger actions or announcements (a major fight, huge hidden fact, slap or punch that wasn't expected, sudden entrance with big news, full-scale evacuation, wedding cancelled, etc.).

Whenever someone drops a bomb, you need to see the crater. If you hear a director say "You missed a beat" or "the stakes aren't high enough/clear enough", often it is not the actor doing the action that is the problem, it's the responder/listener/crowd who failed to register the severity of the impact. I like to think of it as bombs and craters. At its most extreme, if someone important enters, it is the ensemble on stage that can make that matter or not. The actor who is doing the entering can only do so much. The actor revealing a secret has limited tools. It is the other players on stage who create the status or build the dramatic intensity through appropriate physical, vocal, and emotionally active ensemble reactions.

Big ideas in small spaces

This is a Lecoq exercise that helps people consider space usage more effectively.

Action

In groups of two to three, stage a chase scene in which a robber or robbers has escaped into the forest, with one to two cops close behind. The challenge is to stage the whole chase scene constrained to a 4 × 8 platform. The robber fleeing must enter the space, and then use body language/mime to crawl through brush, climb over obstacles, go into caves, or climb up trees with the cop in hot pursuit. Get separated. Hide. Have the cop find you, kill, or be killed. You can dig tunnels, plant traps, any actions that the audience can see and follow from beginning to end without ever leaving the 4 × 8 platform. Notice how easily the audience suspends their disbelief. It is much more fun to believe there are robbers waving across a canyon at each other from a treetop with a cop in a canoe below than it is to believe it is three actors standing on a 4 × 8 platform.

Whether the cop or bandit wins is immaterial, what matters is how well they establish a believable world, and carry the audience along, giving the illusion that they are in a vast landscape, sometimes with great distances or heights between them, yet always staying within a few actual feet of each other, if not literally on top of each other. It is amazing how well this works on the imagination of an audience, and it is a valuable tool that comes into play when developing full-length pieces.

Tabletop theater

Find ways to use objects, gestures, and puppetry to suggest natural disasters, film imagery, or scenes from a novel on an even smaller stage: a tabletop.

Action

Give yourself a huge event to stage, like the destruction of New Orleans from Hurricane Katrina or the Battle of Gettysburg. Figure out a way to suggest it on a card table, using paper, string, tape, and other simple objects, combined with accompanying text or music. A sensitivity to the movement of objects can be acquired through practice. An awareness of the narrative quality of objects in action, done at the right time and with the right dialogue, can produce wonderful results. It can be satirical in tone, like the shows of Paul

Zaloom,[4] or lyrical, such as the work of Basil Twist,[5] who staged the Symphonie Fantastique with fabric moving through a tank of water.

Two of the best moments of theatrical magic Beau Jest ever made involved objects: the Little Brick Dance in the middle of *Krazy Kat*, an homage to Chaplin's dinner roll dance,[6] and the "grass in the wind" moment in *Samurai 7.0*.[7] Find objects or materials that make sense for the world you are creating, and spend a few nights playing with them on stage. Play large, play small, play with music and with text. See what comes up. Choreograph it. Be obsessive. I read that when Kurosawa shot the scene we were echoing, he had the entire field spray painted a certain color so that the reeds looked exactly as he wanted them to on film in the moonlight. Once you know the effect you want to create, go for it.

Dance prompts

There are many kinds of choreographic exercises and etudes useful for actors doing ensemble work. It is beyond the scope of this book to go into them in detail, but I would just like to mention a few of my favorites, used by many different dance companies and choreographers.

Stop & go

Action

Groups of any size. Take a starting position in the space. Someone outside the group says "go". Everyone moves until the "director" says "stop". Everyone is responsible for remembering exactly what they did, being definitive with their actions, and able to repeat it from position one to position two. The director then says "go" again, and "stop" after a few more seconds of material, and so on. Continue for 10 to 12 phrases. At any time someone is confused, go back to one and repeat actions until you can "learn" the choreography you are inventing. End by running the whole piece without pausing, but hitting each point as a group as the piece proceeds.

This is a great exercise for learning to move with clarity and conviction. By stopping and going, it also gives you a chance to see where you are in space in relation to others. Encourage lifts, weight work, counterpoint, floor work, and as the piece develops, if anyone's timing is off and they get somewhere "early", just have them pause till others catch up, then continue. Adjust accordingly. Once the piece is "written", allow for small changes, discussed as a group, so that transitions and momentum can be strengthened.

Three moves

Action

One of the simplest ways to build a dance sequence, which I often use to get a piece started, is to put people into groups of four or five, and ask each actor to create three gestures or phrases inspired by the theme you are exploring. They should be clear and repeatable, and simple enough that they can be taught to the others in the group. Once each actor has three "pieces", they teach them to the group, which means a group of four will then have 12 phrases to string together. The bulk of the work is then putting those pieces in an order that feels right, knowing that you can repeat anything, change the tempo, or invent "connecting" phrases to make them flow together. After about an hour's worth of work your group will have a piece of choreography to bring back to the group to perform. This gesture string can then be performed with different pieces of music, with different tempos, or manipulated by placing it into different contexts.

Scott Graham of Frantic Assembly did a very interesting demonstration in a workshop I took with him in London. He had two actors repeat a 12-part string of gestures while changing small variables. Scott prompted one actor to look away from the other, then have both actors look at the audience, then added a third person circling the pair from outside, and so on. It soon became very clear that the same piece of material could take on vastly different meanings when the context was changed. If you read the Frantic Assembly book on Devising, there is a great discussion about how they develop functional movements and then change the circumstances to create meaning, rather than inventing movement specifically for one purpose in a scene. He often has actors create a gesture string using a certain prompt, without telling them how they will be used in performance.

Variations

Take all the groups and combine them. If you have three different "dances" with groups of four actors each, begin by finding a transition from group one to group two and from group two to group three. Perform the dances in a sequence as if they were meant to lead into each other. Then take all of the best parts of each dance and combine them: speed them up, change the order, create entrances and exits for people until you have a new, hybrid dance for 12 people using some of the material from everyone's exploration that day. Change counts and choreography to adjust it to the size of the ensemble you are ultimately creating for, and create a new opening number or closing finale to the day. Do it once through learning it with slow music, then speed it up and try it again with a high-energy piece of music.

Mark Morris

I took a choreography workshop with the dancer Mark Morris,[8] who had some great structures for making material and teaching dancers a disciplined way of using time, space, movement, and critiques. Here are some of the structures he used.

Make a dance based on your first performance in front of people:

- Recreate the first time you ever performed for an audience;
- Take what is essential and important in that movement and amplify it;
- Put the dance in one plane, like an Egyptian hieroglyph, and get as much of the piece as possible into the space without leaving that line.

Make a war dance:

- The piece is five measures long, in five/four time;
- You have five dancers;
- Pick one element to accent;
- You have five minutes.

Make a canon (a dance phrase everyone learns and performs out of sequence with each other, each dancer starting four beats after the other, like a round in music):

- Use four dancers;
- Create a floor pattern that is all curves;
- Each phrase is four bars long;
- Set it as a canon that can repeat forever;
- Add in doing it in reverse, or retrograde.

Do a dance based on the Four Seasons:

- Four people in a group;
- Each person handles one season;
- Twenty minutes for each section;
- Each choreographer connects to the ending action of the previous part;
- You can choose to be in your section or not.

Make a fantasy dance:

- All sounds/music must be produced by the actors;
- Must be from a time other than now;
- In a place other than here, of which you have no knowledge.

Choreograph a dance for six people entirely on paper. Describe in detail with words only, no diagrams, what you want the dancers to do. Fit all of the directions for the dance onto one page. Don't put your name on it. Give the paper to the dancers, and go away. Give them an hour to create the dance using the instructions. Watch it, and see how clear your instructions were in communicating the dance you wanted them to do.

Probably the most powerful lesson in that workshop was Mark's method of preparation and eye for detail. For preparation, it was simple. If we were about to present pieces, Mark would ask someone to go. If they got up and stalled for any reason, or apologized, or tried to explain something, he'd just ask them to sit back down and ask someone else to go who was ready. It seemed a bit ruthless at first, but it actually just helped make people more definitive in their actions and kept the focus on the work. It kept everyone in an energized state of being ready to go – always – and let the work speak for itself.

In analysis, Mark always asked everyone to first just say what they saw, in the order that they saw it, in as accurate and as detailed a way as possible. This is an incredibly useful exercise, and very difficult to do at first until you get some practice at it. Visual artists use this tool as well when looking at a painting: simply try to say what you see. If someone tried to insert a value judgment, Mark would stop them immediately and ask them to just describe what they saw, with no opinion. For instance, he stopped one participant who said, "next they did those abstract arm movements", and he said, "what do you mean abstract? I saw them all, they looked very real to me, what are you trying to say?" This was a revelatory remark. Participants soon learned to just talk through a piece, as a group, with anyone adding in detail others forgot, so that a complete picture of the dance was recreated after each presentation. At that point, suggestions are made for improvements. Sometimes they came from Mark, sometimes from other participants, usually along the lines of keeping what was most exciting, and changing what seemed least memorable. The more we did it, the better we got at talking about movement, about building our visual memory, and about trusting each other to accurately describe what we saw.

Pilobolus

I spent a week in a choreography workshop with Jonathan Wolken, one of the founders of the physical theater/dance troupe Pilobolus.[9] There were 20 of us, and we worked in a huge, open church hall on the coast of Maine. Jonathan's favorite thing to do was to put on a piece of music in the morning and just encourage people to move and discover spontaneous bits of invention. While we were moving, Jonathan would signal some new technique to try out: low center of gravity; no gratuitous spinning or arm swinging; quick changes in direction; no ambiguous "noodling", as he called it; soft contact converted into shared weight whenever you collided with someone; keeping an eye out for forming interesting patterns in the room with others; allowing the popcorn effect to take over (one person triggering another); playing out duets or trios when they occurred and giving space to others to do the same without piling on and smothering it. He liked to play music loudly, and it was always an invigorating way to spend the day. This is a very useful thing to do with an ensemble, a class, or a workshop every now and then. Just allow for a couple of hours of vigorous dance, play, and improvisation with no theme. In this kind of a massive movement jam, many instincts sharpened while muscle tone and stamina are being built, and greater spatial awareness, risk-taking, and weight-bearing work is a natural outcome.

When it did come time to shape ideas into pieces, Jonathan's prompts were often very simple:

- a duet, picking one gesture or action to explore together with full commitment;
- a group of five using everyday actions as the vocabulary of the piece;
- three people doing something in precise unison.

His critiques for improving a piece often boiled down to using his fingers to mime scissors snipping a piece of film when the group feedback made clear that something was too long and needed editing, or isolating the two to three elements that seemed to be at the heart of a piece, and asking that the participants focus on that more and cut the rest.

Pilobolus initially choreographed all of their pieces using group consensus. Often disagreement was a part of the process, but the investment by all dancers, and the willingness to speak up and try things led to a unique company dynamic that continues to evolve. Eventually the founding artistic directors of the company began to delegate, and different pieces were choreographed by specific individuals. After that, new companies emerged as Moses Pendelton, Alison Chase, and Martha Clarke left the company to pursue their own careers and begin other troupes.

4 *Large Prompts*

The prompts in this chapter require more rehearsal, more feedback, and more rounds of development. They lead to pieces that can stand on their own in performance. All of this work is best developed with an outside eye or practice audience. If you have an ensemble of eight people, work in groups of four so that one group can observe the other group's work. If you have an odd number like nine, you might try different-sized groups: one group of four, a trio and a duet, and so on. If you are in a classroom or workshop, divide into groups that make the most sense with the numbers you have. If you have an ensemble of five, work as a group, and then have someone sit outside the group to watch the results or bring a trusted eye in to watch the work as it progresses. Rotate who sits out, or try working with a video camera so you can all see what you are doing. This does *not* mean show the results to a paying audience. These exercises are building blocks focused on developing a process that can yield performable material. They are not necessarily entertainment forms on their own. It is often a messy process, disjointed and full of unfinished possibilities. Keep this work in the studio where it can proceed unimpeded until you have a piece you consider a "finished" work you want to present to a real audience. That being said, many of these prompts do make for very entertaining pieces. Feedback from a real audience can help you develop it a step further. You may also want to have a person introduce the work or a program note explaining the origin of the material if it helps to frame for an audience what they are seeing.

Paragraphs

Action
Find a descriptive paragraph from a novel of your choosing. Make sure it has language that is rich in imagery, character, ideas, or action. Get into groups of four to five, read the paragraph out loud, and then spend a couple of hours trying to translate it into an event on stage.

This *does not* mean acting out the paragraph as literally as possible. You can evoke the mood of the words, use the text as narration with counterpointed imagery, or develop a translation of the essence of the paragraph into a scene that echoes its emotional or intellectual content. Add music if needed, or props/materials to create the world.

You can present your piece by reading the paragraph aloud and then performing it, or do your version and then read the paragraph that inspired it afterwards. Both methods have value. Ultimately, the source of the original material is less important than the new work of art you create. In fact, it is good practice to try unlocking the literal meaning and think freely about what you can do with it on stage. For example:

Variation

Have one group work on a paragraph for an hour or two from one source, and another group develop a piece on a completely different paragraph. Keep the work physical, focusing on gestures, movements, and actions inspired by the words, but do not use any text out loud when developing your piece. Once you have your movement piece finished, trade paragraphs, and see what happens when you present your piece while reading the words from a different paragraph layered on top. Sometimes, the results are remarkable. Gesture patterns found through one story will highlight different meanings in the text of the other story.

Next, make it more intentional. Teach your piece to the other group, and learn theirs. *Then* add both texts, so that the linkage between gesture and language is more complex. Adjust slightly whatever movements have to be made in order to use as much of the text from both paragraphs as you want. You need not say every word. Inevitably, audiences will impose their own meaning. People watching will be amazed by how well the actions developed by one group suit the text from another group. This is an important step in training the body how *not* to just reiterate in movement what is being said already vocally. But again, it is not devoid of meaning, and this exercise is meant to develop a deeper appreciation of the physical possibilities of juxtaposition and surprise, like composition in a good painting, as opposed to plain, representational actions. Because you are mashing up two different sources, surprise and unpredictable results are a given.

Paragraph variations

It isn't much of a leap to go from paragraph work to telling larger stories. My advice is to work in manageable bites. First, take one paragraph or a small section of a story and practice using a range of theatrical devices to express it: monologues, songs, dance sequences, puppets, scene study, narrators, collage, etc. Try some of these interpretive variations:

- Treat the paragraph as a musical theater number;
- Turn it into a solo monologue;
- Do it as a monologue with one person speaking off stage and one person moving with/against the text on stage;
- Do it as a puppet show;
- Use video- and music-editing software or digital media to turn it into a mediated piece;
- Make it a pure dance sequence with no language;
- Present it as a pure language piece, with no action on stage, using stationary bodies to deliver the text in choral fashion, or into microphones;
- Create a state of sensory overload by doing two or three of these approaches at the same time.

Once you have explored these options, you should have more devising tools available and a better sense of what method will work best for transforming any given story to the stage.

Stories

Now take a story that interests you from a magazine, a book, something you've heard, or something that happened to you, and make some artistic choices. What is the best way to interpret this story? Should it be a mash-up of styles? Does it have a serious tone or a sparseness you want to reflect throughout the whole piece? Does it have twists and turns that call out for a surprising puppet sequence, a musical number, a video fantasy sequence? Does it need music? Light? Objects? A big production number? Think outside the box. If possible, give two different groups the same story to work with for a couple of days, then get back together and compare the results. No one will ever capture everything in a story in the same way, and each group will highlight different narrative elements. Some may have a stronger opening, others an exciting climactic sequence. This practice is what will, in the end, help you to define your artistic voice. And seeing other people's choices helps broaden one's thinking.

Here are a few prompts for approaching a larger project by using smaller "bites". These tools also work when adapting a script, a film, novels, or plays.

Images

Action

To begin, break the story into a series of images. Spend time developing a treatment for each important scene. Start with the four to five most important moments in the story. Spend a couple hours working on the images or narrative possibilities that interest the group, and then show them to someone else. Then start using the following beginning, middle, and end exercises.

Beginnings

Action

Brainstorm three different beginnings. Spend only an hour or two in rehearsal to find them. Try something logical, and something totally out there. Present all three versions to an outside eye or other people for feedback. Often, the best way to begin will be apparent, and the other two choices can be folded in for later use, edited out, or integrated into the opening.

Middles

Action

Focus on the central conflict. What key images and narrative points have to be in the story? Work the middle conflict without worrying about how you get there, or how it ends. Really flesh out the action, make it exciting, and bring out the drama or humor that attracted you to the story in the first place.

Endings

Action

Find what payoff your version of the story has set the audience up for. Try two or three alternative endings. Should it shock? Suspend? Give a sense of full closure? End with a fade-out, a blackout, a song, or a dance? Present the whole piece, and run it each time for outside eyes with a different ending. Which is most satisfying? Get feedback from the audience/viewers, and incorporate any suggestions that make sense.

Translations

Action

Open up the possibilities by creating a translation of the event. You can play out a completely different scene than the one described in the story, as long as it captures something truthful about the psychology or essence of the original. Take the same central conflict, and do a translation of it. Think up a similar scene using a different location and set of characters, and stage it by translating the story into a different world. On a grand scale, *West Side Story* is a translation of *Romeo and Juliet.* You can practice translations by taking something simple, like Aesop's Fable of the *Fox and the Grapes,* and think up a parallel situation. If the setting were an office or a factory, how would that story translate? At the core of many contemporary tales you will find variations on an old story like *The Boy Who Cried Wolf* or *The Emperor's New Clothes*.

Love/hate

Action

Include two things in your piece:

- something you feel has to be in the piece (that you would love to perform);
- something you would hate to have in the piece (because it is too corny, obvious, cliché, stupid, or beyond your skills).

Present both, without saying which is which. Often, the audience will find value in both. Incorporating both will make for a richer piece.

Foreground/background

Action

Intentionally do something using two planes for staging. Play two events at the same time that may or may not relate to each other. Do something downstage at the same time something different is going on upstage. Focus on how to present both in the space as a unified composition, creating spatial depth and complexity so that the audience can see both events in one unified frame. Be aware of how the timing in the upstage event affects the perception of the downstage event, and whether it is distracting or intriguing.

Index cards or post-its

Action

Take all of your images, experiments, great ideas, and lousy ideas and work on the arrangement. It need not be a chronological telling. One method is to put every improvisation, bit of dialogue, image, song, or topic on an index card or post-it note. Partly this is to remember what you have done, and it allows you to experiment with different arrangements. You can string up a clothesline and pin the cards on it in the order you want to try out, or lay them out on the floor in different sequences. Use your instinct to try different orders, and see what each provokes. Or you can organize them by categories – dance sequences, monologues, visual images, prop/object studies – and try combining two or three of them in a collage. Over time, the ideas that keep popping back up become the backbone of a piece, and the things that don't seem to fit, or feel right but in the wrong place, end up on the back burner or in another show.

The spine

You have probably noticed by now that working on a story complicates the work of making decisions as a group. Larger prompts have more forks in the road, and you need an organizing principle to guide the work. This is where having a *spine* is useful (a term I first heard used by the director Harold Clurman, in his book *On Directing*).[1]

Action

Read or say the story out loud. Discuss as an ensemble and agree on what is most important: what is the spine of this piece? This is extremely important, especially when you are feeling lost in the woods and need to find true north. Before giving up, define a spine; it will lead you to clarity. Regardless of the story's specific narrative events, is it about Coping with Loss? Defying All Odds? The Limits of Intimacy? Family Secrets? Getting Away from It All? The Power of Forgiveness? Decide how you want to focus the story, then build your imagery and narrative ideas off of that spine. Make sure everything serves the spine and edit out extraneous events or ideas. Repeat it like a mantra when feeling lost.

Epic tales in short times

Action

Choose a well-known story or film. Spend an afternoon creating a condensed version of the whole film or story, capturing the essence of the original. Find interesting visual solutions to the signature scenes everyone knows. Work with perspective shifts, language, music, text, and movement to capture the story or film in three to ten minutes. Again, the short time limit is there to provoke bold problem solving. Signature lines of dialogue can be treated as choral material underscoring other events. An action scene that begins with real people can dissolve into impressionistic imagery sampled from throughout the novel or film. Find a way to compress events or turn the entire story into a poetic collage. You can use music, props, dialogue, costumes – whatever comes to mind when you start working. The piece does not need to be rushed: just inventive. There can be moments of stillness and suspense, boredom, and intrigue, using sampling and compression to get at the heart of the story in a shorter time frame. I've seen *The Wizard of Oz* captured without using any dialogue, and *Uncle Tom's Cabin* played as a puppet show with characters made from trash. Be creative.

Everyone in the group should read or watch the source material so that image and dialogue choices are informed. Many of the earlier exercises in physical imagery, contact improvisation, counterbalance, group sculptures, and dynamics of nature are useful for this work. People can be smoke, fog, rain, forests, chasms, voids, different time periods, or multiple characters. Any choice, from *Alice in Wonderland*

and *The Lord of the Rings* to *Tom Sawyer* and *The Seventh Seal* will
work, as long as it is material well known to the group and with visual
possibilities. In-depth psychological studies are much harder to
compress, although you might be able to do an interesting
ten-minute mash-up of Jane Austen or Anton Chekhov, for example.
The interiority of these sources is an advanced devising challenge.
Really doing justice to a complex novel or psychologically rich text
takes months and requires a full-length time frame, which isn't the
point of this exercise. This prompt helps actors develop a sense of
compression and poetic juxtaposition. It also helps an ensemble
determine what is essential in a story, and develops the group's ability
to reach consensus and incorporate many of the earlier physical
exercises in this book. Ensemble skills developed using this prompt
can then be applied to full-length pieces, as described in a later
chapter.

Myths

Myths are extremely rich sources for inspiration. For centuries, scripts
and theatrical adaptations have used myths, timeless stories from
different cultures with universal appeal. Mythic sources influenced the
writing of Eugene O'Neill's *Mourning Becomes Electra* and Julie
Taymor's *The Lion King*. Lookingglass Theater's[2] recent adaption of
Ovid's *Metamorphosis* has been staged by numerous theaters around
the world. Ralph Lee's Mettawee Theater Company[3] tours every
summer with annual productions using myth and folktales
exclusively, from Native American stories, Incan tales, and African,
European, and Indian Myths. Myths are at the root of many theatrical
traditions, from opera and dance to puppetry and storytelling. The
American theater company PigPen used shadow puppetry, acting,
and original music to create a delightfully mythic tale, *The Old Man
and The Old Moon*. I would like to focus on just one key use of myth
that I find particularly helpful for ensemble devising. Myths are a
great way to begin doing site-specific work. I learned about this
approach from Libby Marcus, who used it as part of a theater
curriculum she developed at the Boston Latin School and refined
while teaching at Bowdoin College.

Action
Choose a myth. Read it out loud together. Then think of the best
place to stage it that is *not* in a traditional theater space. Should it be
by a lake in the woods? In front of a municipal building? In an
abandoned state hospital? On a sports field? In a swimming pool?
Using groups of five to six, spend a few hours staging your version of

the story in a found space, making use of all the ways the site can inform the meaning of the myth. Build simple props, costume it, think about where the audience should be, or whether it should travel. Show the results to other groups, get feedback, and then work with whatever time frame you choose to polish and deepen your story.

The iconography of myths invites the use of masks, shadow screens, music, and other theatrical tools to create mythic imagery. All of these items can easily be moved to found spaces. Myths are also well-served by poor theater techniques, and the challenge of devising something outdoors or in a non-theatrical space helps build an ensemble's problem-solving skills, and everyone's awareness of their relationship to the audience and the meaning inherent in the architecture of the performance space.

Variation

This work can then be translated back into a traditional theater, sometimes incorporating natural elements through a clever design concept, or changing the relationship to the audience using innovative or immersive floor patterns. Take the work you did outside of the theater, and translate it back into a traditional performance space.

This is just one small exercise for what could be a much larger project. All of the exercises in this book can be applied to mythic adaptations, and you can spend weeks, years, or a lifetime turning myths into performance. I mention myths here specifically as a Large Prompt for ensemble devising because of their unique value as source material for moving work out of the theater and into the environment. Myths are also an excellent source for full-length work with universal appeal, and many of the later exercises apply. A single myth may have incarnations in films, novels, and plays, so you will have multiple research sources to work with should you choose to use a myth as a start point for full-length work.

These adaptations can be hugely successful. The Fiasco Theater[4] of New York recently staged a very faithful and stripped down version of Shakespeare's *Cymbeline* (a rather mythic tale), using six actors and a trunk to tell the whole story. The show was revived several times, and led to commissions for other stories. In 2015, Fiasco is presenting a revival of Stephen Sondheim's *Into The Woods* (a fairy tale mash-up with a strong spine and gorgeous music) Off Broadway at the Roundabout Theater. Punchdrunk's *Sleep No More*[5] is successful in part because of its use of mythic imagery and the sense of a personal journey into another world that is viscerally disturbing and illuminating.

The Shakespeare project

Action

Form a trio, choose one play by Shakespeare to work with, and make a ten-minute piece out of it. You can capture the essence of the play's central conflicts and language, or create a totally impressionistic event that has little resemblance to the original. The goal is not to speed though the whole play. It is to make a wholly original new piece that is fed by the source material, with the end product being a deep reflection on the nature of the original and the desires of the trio as art makers.

I love this exercise. The muscularity of Shakespeare's language and the imaginative possibilities it provokes are eye-opening. The ten-minute limit is just a guideline for giving people a method for creating a short piece, and for learning the value of compressing or expanding time and space more than the playwright did in the original. Many of the trios I have seen could easily extend their work into the creation of a full-length piece using the same methods without the time limit.

Step One: Go off and work on three possible beginnings. If need be, you can prompt people to vary their choices – something physical and non-literal, something text-based, something using objects; something from the beginning of the play, a start point from the end, a moment with no one on stage, etc. – but I rarely do. People are inevitably more creative than anything I could dream up. And nine times out of ten, all of that material ends up being recycled elsewhere in the piece. Present and get feedback. Go back for one more round of development on these three choices or on one choice that people felt was most promising.

Step Two: Three different uses of language. Think about what lines have to be in your piece, what text would you love to work with? Don't worry about how it is used, in what order, whether you play a specific scene, if a different character speaks it. Try different ways of speaking – choral, unison, echo, monologue, dialogue fragments, shared lines – get it on the table while still working with movement choices. Present all three possibilities and get feedback.

Step Three: Each member of the trio should think about one thing they would love to see/do in this piece, and one thing they would hate to see/do in the piece. In rehearsal, act out/create all six moments. Put them all together and present them. Do not tell the audience which moment is which. Find a way to connect them, in an order that makes sense to you, so that it plays as one unified event. Present and get feedback.

Step Four: Make sure you have the thing you *must* have in your piece in there (Figure 4.1).

Figure 4.1: As You Like It*: Shakespeare Project, Devising Intensive (Sarah Chalfie and Della Moustachella), Celebration Barn, 2014. Photo: Scott Vlaun*

Step Five: Put it all together with a beginning, middle, and end, using some or all of the material you have presented so far. Bring the whole piece in to show, get feedback. Viewers should let the group know if anything they cut or left out was missed, if anything new put in was worth developing, and if the overall order, dialogue, and imagery worked for them.

Step Six: Add counterpoint. Think of it in terms of Ugly, Beautiful, Ordinary, Extraordinary, and make sure you have contrasting moments. Discuss any opportunities for gesture that are non-narrative but add to the emotional impact. Take the feedback, and go off and rehearse one more time before the final presentation.

Mash-ups: The piece you have to make

Two actors are given the following list of challenges.

- Maintain a new physicality: Something that is rare for you. Stay with it for a minimum of two minutes, with ease. It can be within a scene, a musical number, a dance sequence, or in silence.
- Play the scene you have to play.
- Include a phrase of aching beauty.
- An image expressing a huge fear of yours.
- Change and be changed by the performance.
- One line of Shakespeare's verse.

Action

Each actor must fulfill all parts of the exercise. You do not need to play complete scenes. You can do more than one scene. Be supporting actors in each other's scenes. Make interesting transitions and treat the whole piece as a unified event. You can combine Beauty, Fear, and New Physicality into one scene, or treat them as separate phrases. Be brave. It can be realistic or not. Play in any style. Make sure both actors meet all challenges.

This is an advanced list exercise. If you have slumped shoulders, then somewhere in the piece you need to maintain a different physicality for at least two minutes. If doing a musical scares you, then add a musical number. If you have always wanted to play Maggie from *Cat on a Hot Tin Roof*, then do one of her scenes. Meanwhile, your partner, who is always erect and bounces when he walks, must also find a new physicality. Perhaps he is playing Brick to your Maggie. And if you love musicals but are afraid of Shakespeare, help your partner in their musical sequence and then transition into a scene from *The Tempest*. I have seen this prompt solved many ways, including doing a scene from a play straight-up that meets all the requirements for both actors, with a line from Shakespeare dropped in at the appropriate moment (there is always a line that works). I've also seen two actors do amazing mash-ups, like combining a scene from *The Sound of Music* (with a large man playing Maria and a petite woman playing Mother Superior), segueing into a monologue from *Long Day's Journey Into Night*, a brief scene from *Richard II*, a hilarious interlude of meta-theater with each actor imitating the other in rehearsal ending with a musical finale singing *How Do You Solve a Problem Like Maria?*

Variations

Mash-ups as a form have many variations. In part a result of the easy access we now have to video files, audio files, and editing software, sampling work from different sources and cultures and combining them has become a new norm for contemporary art makers. It is too big a topic to go into here, but it is certainly a structure that many devising ensembles work with.

The personal

Action

Make short, original pieces using personal experiences, ideas, and observations. Break into groups of two, three, or four, depending on the nature of the idea. Do some improvising and scripting, and present the pieces back to each other.

The short format is easy to work in. An idea can be fleshed out in a week or two, and an evening of short pieces can be created and presented as an ensemble in as few as six to eight weeks. Add more people into each piece as needed. Short pieces help you to develop writing abilities, a performance aesthetic, and an identity as an ensemble. Using personal experience as material opens you up to both comic and dramatic terrain. Ideas can be expressed as stories, puppet shows, dances, music – whatever you personally need to do. Some ideas may have potential for further development as a full-length project.

The short format is both a blessing and a curse. It is an easy way to start devising, but it sometimes becomes a trap that is hard to break out of. The cultural tendency is to think of the material as inherently comic, but if your initial work is more serious or dance oriented, you can nip that expectation in the bud. Once you are accustomed to short pieces, it is harder to conceive of longer works. Full-length pieces require a very different rehearsal process with much more planning, writing, thought, and time. The next chapter discusses the development of full-length pieces, but I would like to say a few things about the value of smaller ideas first.

Making short, original pieces is an inherently democratic process. You don't need to agree on a grand vision to get started. If someone wants to make a dance using a certain piece of music and only one other person is interested, make it a duet. If no one wants to join in, you have a solo. If someone has a story or theme that everyone wants to work on, images, ideas, and dialogue can be developed collaboratively. Structure can be imposed democratically, or someone acting as a final editor or director can be the outside eye who shapes it. Depending on the make-up of your ensemble, you may have a writer who wants to script something and bounce it off the group, or you may have a musician who has an idea for a new song or vocal arrangement. In other words, you don't need a unified, collective vision of what your work is before you start. You just devise material that takes advantage of your ensemble's unique talents in smaller bites. Soon you will have a number of short pieces, and your company's point of view will begin to emerge. Put the pieces in some kind of order, work out transitions, give it a title you can publicize, and you have a show.

Beau Jest's first show was a collage of personal observations. We staged some of the frustrations of city life, going to work, shopping, difficulties in relationships, and brief moments of fantasy fulfillment. This was not the stuff of a major piece, but the attention to detail and development of image-making skills along the way were important building blocks for our vocabulary as an ensemble in later full-length work. Reflecting on these experiences became an enjoyable and entertaining way of holding a mirror up to our own natures. Poetic physical transitions became a part of our vocabulary. Soon a style emerged which, for lack of a better word, was Beau Jest-ian. People started to tell us, "I saw this show you would like, it was very Beau Jest." Working on small pieces gave us the tools we needed to take on larger themes and more complex, full-length work.

If your ensemble doesn't have a clear idea of what work you want to make, try making an evening of shorter pieces. Many good ideas aren't worth a full hour of stage time, and it may take a while working together to develop a shared aesthetic and a vision. You may find one or two members need to drop out, or new people need to be added. Our work with short pieces helped us develop a lyrical, physical method of storytelling and stretched our ability to find imaginative solutions. Short pieces let you create in manageable bites and present work while developing your identity as an ensemble.

Sometimes, the careful arrangement of short pieces can become a cohesive full-length piece. Bill Irwin's[6] breakthrough show, *The Regard of Flight*, was carefully scripted using several older pieces that came out of years of clowning with the Pickle Family Circus in California. His hit show on Broadway with David Shiner, *Fool Moon*, was a very savvy merging of both performer's solo material and the lively music of the Red Clay Ramblers. Their latest reprise of that partnership, *Old Hats*, used solo material and some newly created duets to weave everything together in an aesthetically pleasing order with the added magic of Nellie McKay's live music and charming persona as a third partner counterbalancing the relationship of "the boys". Recycling old material in new forms is a time-honored tradition by artists of all stripes, including ensemble devisers.

5 Organizational Structures

Before doing any full-length work, you'll need to make sure your group is organized. Here are some common organizing structures for ensembles. Some of these models exist in the professional theater, some are used in the classroom or a workshop, and some grow out of short- or long-term necessity. Any group that lasts more than a year probably has agreed on a structure. If you are in an in-class project, do what you must to make it through the semester and complete the assignment. Decide who handles what workload, and try to make sure work is distributed fairly.

First is an exercise that allows you to experience several typical management structures, to help you get a taste for which way your ensemble prefers to work.

Working methods

Action

Do a controlled experiment. Make a five-minute piece with the title Vacations. Work for a half hour with one method listed below, and present it. Then start over, using another method on the same theme with the same time limit. Present it. Do it again with each method. Try each structure and see which works best for your group. You may decide to use all five methods when you make a piece, or stick to one. Having an awareness of these methods may help when you reach a creative impasse.

- *Yes, and . . .* : Do everything anyone proposes. Make sure everyone puts in at least one idea, and there is no saying no. *Everything* proposed gets done. The only answer to someone saying "let's go to the beach at Coney Island" is "yes, and . . . we see mermaids dancing in the waves", etc. Do it, no matter how hard an idea it may be to execute or how random the narrative may seem to you.
- *Rotate leadership*: Each person leads one section of the work. Choose whether they want to be in it or not. Person A directs the opening scene, person B does the middle action, person C

choreographs the dance, and person D handles the ending. All four work together on the transitions, and each "director" can decide how their section begins.

- *Choose a director*: Decide on one person to direct the whole piece. Let them structure the rehearsal and the choices made. Others can have input, but in the end, the director decides.
- *Assign roles*: Decide who will create the dramatic structure, who will write the dialogue, who will choreograph, who will be the outside eye.
- *Debate and vote*: Work as a group, but allow differences to be expressed. Debate every choice, majority rules.

It's worth trying each of these systems, because people tend to default to the system they are most comfortable with. Experimenting with different methods help natural "leader" types learn to let go of control, and "follower" types to get comfortable taking charge.

Academic needs

Schools teach devising a variety of ways. A teacher or director may lead the work, or students may have free rein to make all the decisions. If faculty guide all the work, students will never have a chance to learn how to lead. If faculty impose no order, students will have no model for ways to proceed. The best programs give students an introduction to various existing models of ensemble structure, and opportunities to develop their own artistic voices through a progression of challenges that give them an opportunity to try, fail, and try again until they find the devising process and leadership models that work best for them. This can range from semester-long classes or projects to professional-level work guided by a guest artist. Ambitious students can lead year-long thesis projects that may include a year of research and dramaturgy before rehearsals begin. If you are teaching devising, give your students some projects that are specifically focused on power dynamics in a group, and ask them to experience two or three of these models in depth. And students need time, guidance, reflection, and prodding to be encouraged to find themselves as devising artists.

Professional needs

Professional companies need to figure out how to sustain their activities. Some might establish a five-year business plan with a professional manager, development staff, an active board, and clearly defined jobs while developing artistic projects. Or they might just bounce along as a group with an informal daily check-in routine and a free place to rehearse. Either way, it is important to recognize how decisions get made and agree on the organizational structure that is best for your ensemble. You need to come up with a plan for how to pay for the ensemble's work. You need to find places to rehearse, salaries for performers, and money for production expenses. You need a process for reaching consensus on what the company wants to work on next. Most groups forming a permanent company take the legal step of becoming a corporation (easy), and filing for non-profit 501(c) 3 status as a cultural organization with the federal government (harder) so that they can fundraise and apply for grants. These steps require a mission statement, the formation of a board of directors, and elected positions of governance spelled out in the company's by-laws.

Let's look at how decisions get made and who makes them. Regardless of your academic, professional, or legal status, the day-to-day work of making theater together usually falls into one of these standard models:

- actors/designers *led by an artistic director*;
- actors/designers *collaborating with one to two writers/creators*;
- democratic *collective* – no leaders, all vote, consensus rules;
- *rotating outside eyes* – one person watches and is in charge of a section or project, different leaders or directors for different tasks.

If there is no leader, devising can be a long, turbulent process with conflicting artistic opinions and no agreement on how decisions get made. This is one of the more infuriating aspects of devising. When personalities clash and there is a lack of goodwill, devising work can be emotionally exhausting. The dynamics change considerably when an ensemble hires an outside eye or director/writer to guide the work. If there is trust, this can save a lot of time. This is probably the ideal format for making new work. The downside of this model is when there is a lack of trust, or outright animosity against the leader, people will do the work but tensions and resentments will disrupt the working atmosphere and open communication gets lost. You may have experienced this pattern where a leader was difficult to work with but the company ended up bonding and making a great piece. Collectives (where everything is argued out as a group) have their own pluses and minuses too. Here is a closer look at group dynamics, and some tips for how to save time while working together.

Models

Tossed in the pool together

This is the structure most often used in classroom settings. It also happens in professional workshops when strangers are tossed together at random on an assignment and find great joy and creativity working together in brief, energetic bursts. Leadership overlaps, and time pressures usually keep arguments brief so that solutions can be arrived at communally. Later on, people go back to their own homes, jobs, or classes, but in that moment a new ensemble is born. It's a great way to work on short-term ideas. And throwing people together in a random group on a project sometimes leads to groups staying together and forming new ensembles after leaving the workshop or classroom. The dance troupe Pilobolus began this way when students in a dance class at Dartmouth College made a piece together, found an aesthetic they were all excited by, and ended up forming a troupe that pulled their dance teacher away from her college job to join them as they created a new troupe and began their careers.

Tossed in the pool is an effective way for people to learn to work together, to negotiate differences, and to produce under a deadline. There is nothing better than giving a group of people a daunting challenge and a time limit. With some assignments, 15 minutes is enough time to go out of the room and come back with a short piece to present. This generates excitement and sometimes frustration, but the time pressure helps resolve differences and is a great motivator for getting things done. Everyone starts as equals, there is usually a good-natured, tentative willingness that quickly picks up steam as one idea fires off another and the collective imagination takes hold. Results are often miraculous. This structure can be used for extended assignments as well, with a task that takes three to four weeks to fulfill. Build in a couple of check-in points for presenting the work for feedback and suggestions every week. Within a month, a complex 15-minute piece can result. I've seen students do this freshman year who fondly recall their ensemble project four years later. The work they made and the bond formed during that process of creating an original piece together is often mentioned as one of the highlights of their college career. While there may be natural leaders who emerge in these settings, or peace-makers who help to diffuse tensions, no formal structure is imposed at the outset and the group "sinks or swims" on its own merits.

This structure can also break down, usually for one of the following reasons:

- No one presents any ideas, everyone is resistant to the assignment, and a general reluctance sets in that prevents anything from starting. Comments are usually along the lines of "We couldn't think of anything" or "I don't get what we are supposed to do". *Solution*: Just do something. Any idea is better than nothing.
- One strong personality dominates the group, insisting on doing something that misinterprets the assignment or that no one is interested in. Out of politeness or fear, the others go along rather

than openly disagree, and the group runs out of time with a half-staged, dysfunctional idea that only one person was committed to trying. *Solution*: Speak up if you don't agree, and present alternatives. Working as an ensemble means being able to hear different ideas, not just agree on everything. If you can't commit to something, say so, suggest something else, and find a solution.

- There are two or more strong ideas competing in the group at the beginning, and the group runs out of time before exploring either, or finding a way to use both/all ideas. *Solution*: Ask for more time.

- The group gets involved in minutiae, polishing one moment repeatedly or attempting to do something beyond the skill level of the performers in the time allotted, and they never finish the assignment because they only have that one semi-polished moment to present. *Solution*: Have someone keep an eye on the clock, and hold the group to how long they will spend polishing something before calling "Time" and moving on. If it is clear someone's offer is beyond the skill level or time limit of the group, don't do it and stage it poorly. Do *less* well, rather than *more* poorly.

Fortunately, these problems don't occur very often. In general people want to work, and with the right introduction they can produce remarkable work in a short amount of time. If the teacher/leader doesn't tell participants that what they are about to do is impossible or difficult, they often will achieve the impossible and the difficult. Seeing other groups working well together in a big room is also a good motivator.

Another issue arises when players get to know each other. By mid-semester in a class doing this work, or in a company that has been working together for months, patterns emerge and people know who always dominates a group, who never speaks up, who has really bizarre ideas, who seems to keep coming up with "successful" ideas, who is a good performer, who they like to work with, who they want to avoid. This is all natural, and no amount of discussion will change it, but good facilitation and a respectful atmosphere helps. Sometimes people just have strange ideas, limited skills, or are pushy and will always try to get their ideas used. It's a given. The successful groups realize that the goal is to use everyone in the group to *their* best advantage, not get mad at each other for what they can't or won't do. I urge people to try everything, and to realize that it's okay to let go of always getting your own way. See what happens if everyone imagines other people are just as interesting as they are!

A classic dictum for people making work together is: *Work with the group you have, not the group you wish you had.*

My main rule of thumb when leading a devising workshop is to use numbers, names in a hat, or other methods for picking groups at random, and to keep changing the group's members on different projects to avoid cliques and stereotyping. This also helps to level the playing field. When the "cool" group has a dud, or the "quiet" group makes something brilliant, this really helps in a class or workshop situation. People learn to acknowledge differences, learn to speak up when they disagree or can't commit to an idea, and learn to work towards the "greater good" of getting an assignment done. Laziness or not showing up for a rehearsal should be handled by removal from the group, unless it's a health issue or personal emergency.

In this structure, meritocracy prevails. Someone suggests an idea. Someone else suggests another. The one that catches the group's interest usually wins. I coach groups to make a habit of trying all ideas as they are floated. If there is disagreement, it is faster to try both ideas and decide which works best, rather than spend ten minutes debating the pros and cons of both approaches without trying either. Because there is no leader, and everyone needs to be comfortable as performers with the choices made, I also suggest people find their own way to commit to a piece, and do something else when they can't fit into the main action. Enter later, or play a supporting part. You can also try out different power structures.

Groups with a leader

Many professional ensembles have a distinctive style shaped by key members or founders who serve as actual or de facto artistic leaders. They set the tone of the work, choose the next project, have a say in the casting, set the rehearsal process, and define the group's aesthetic. Their work has a recognizable style that people are drawn to. Actors join these groups to work in that style because they find it inspiring and engaging and want to be a part of that company's vision. In joining a group with this structure, you support an aesthetic set by the leaders, contributing when asked but leaving the larger choices up to the directors. Actors in groups such as Theatre De Soleil, Frantic Assembly, SITI Company, The Rude Mechanicals, and The Civilians use this structure. It is probably the most common model, because it works so well organizationally. Often, some form of voice or movement training is part of the daily routine of the company, led either by the founders or by people appointed by the founders. The work tends to have a unified artistic look because one or two people with a strong vision are shaping the final product.

Leaders come in many styles. There are companies with very relaxed leadership styles, or very mysterious and undefined methods. Some have joint leaders, some rotate. A close examination of any group will reveal who is in charge and how an aesthetic is arrived at. In Beau Jest, I am artistic director and make final decisions, but I rely heavily on actors and designers to come up with better ideas than my own. I write on my feet with the help of others, and can't sit down and create a show on my own. I am better at organizing brainstorming sessions and working as an editor and arranger than I am as a structural visionary. When I am acting in a piece, I prefer having a co-director who can see the work from outside and help us shape it.

My leadership style was affected by other ensemble experiences before forming Beau Jest. One was a collective called Amherst Mime Theater that collapsed in its first year of operation (see next topic: collectives). Another was as an actor with The Mettawee Theater Company[1] in upstate New York led by Ralph Lee. Mettawee performs outdoors and works with material that is "mythic". Ralph's partner, Casey, creates all the costumes, and the productions use masks and puppets designed by Ralph. There is a unified aesthetic to all Mettawee shows that is distinctly Ralph and Casey's. While different actors come and go each year, the core vision is remarkably stable. They are about to enter their 40th year as an ensemble.

Ralph is a delightful, humble, and charming man to work with. He is a visionary, who founded New York's Village Halloween Parade. In Mettawee, the direction, the script, the design, and production logistics were Ralph and Casey's concerns. My responsibility was to develop the character I was hired for, to contribute to rehearsals as needed, and to share the workload of set-up, strike, and, on occasion, cook. It is a well-run organization. It was also excellent training for me in how to lead a company. I didn't yet have a strong personal aesthetic I wanted to develop, and I was learning by observing. Watching how Ralph and Casey worked together, how they made a show, and how they helped foster a healthy working atmosphere with everyone living in tight quarters and traveling on the road was a great learning experience. I knew when I started Beau Jest that it was a model I wanted to follow.

One thing Ralph did religiously at every rehearsal and performance was a vocal warm-up. I knew it was a good idea for our voices, being outdoors, but the importance of the warm-up was less about projection and more about a communal routine binding the group together. Ralph was an actor with the seminal Open Theater[2] ensemble led by Joe Chaikin. A part of that legacy was his introduction to Linklater voice work (Kristin worked with the Open

Theater when she first came to the United States). The daily ritual of vocal exercises was something Ralph carried over from his work with Linklater and Chaiken to his work with Mettawee Theater. Ralph led the warm-up, and I would imagine that it is still very much a part of his daily process. I learned to appreciate the value of a company ritual. If you work with Ann Bogart and the SITI Company, Suzuki technique and Viewpoints are part of the glue that holds the company together. They practice their methods daily, whether new to the company or a founding member.

Collective

Some groups try to avoid hierarchical structures. They employ complex methods of daily checking in, and discuss all issues as a group until consensus is reached. This was the structure we used in the first ensemble I was part of after college. I was one of nine actors who met in a summer workshop at the Celebration Barn Theater, where we devised group ensemble pieces and several solo and duet pieces. At the end of the summer nine of us decided to stay together, move to a house in Amherst, Massachusetts, and start our careers as The Amherst Mime Theater. It seemed like it wouldn't be too hard to start booking performances and working on new ideas using our shared vocabulary from training together. Probably the first mistake we made was renting one house together to live in when none of us had money, which meant that issues like how high to keep the thermostat in the winter and who ate the Swiss cheese in the refrigerator crept into the dynamic of the group's rehearsal process. Things became terribly cumbersome as we moved into a theater for our first show and every choice, from where to put the lights to what order to present our pieces, became a major argument. The reality of having no agreed-upon model for resolving disagreements stared us in the face. In the big picture, it probably didn't matter what order the pieces were in or where we hung the lights. We just needed someone to say "let's do it this way" and save the group a lot of misery. We should have foreseen this and discussed a decision-making system before we were in crisis mode.

If you find yourselves in this position, don't be afraid to choose a director, rotate directors, or hire an outside eye. Even the most egalitarian groups have some form of hierarchy in order to get things done. Good art is a meritocracy, not a democracy. The Mark Morris dance group makes brilliant work because Mark is a great choreographer, and he adjusts every hand position and step in every piece. Theatre de Soleil makes brilliant pieces because Arianne Mnouchkine is a brilliant director, and while the company is founded on communal principles, the work is always steered by Mnouchkine.

Not all choices are equal, and the wisest groups find a way to put people with appropriate expertise in charge of each area. It then becomes more about communicating and coordinating instead of debating every step along the way.

In Amherst Mime's only year of operation, all attempts at delegating were seen as an insensitive power grab. Tony Montanaro, our teacher and mentor at the Celebration Barn, wasn't directing us, and no one agreed on who should. While there was a collective spirit at the Celebration Barn where we all met, the work had been guided by an artistic director (Tony), and when we were on our own that central role was unfilled. Tony knew we were going off to start a troupe together and told us it would be like a marriage, so build it on love and care for each other. It was a nice sentiment, but unrealistic. The group was too big, there were too many agendas in the room. After a few shows together the group fractured into solo artists, clowning duos, an actor going into radio and television work, and a few who formed a new ensemble. I decided privately whatever group I was involved in next, it would have an artistic director and a clear structure for how decisions got made.

Co-directors

Some groups – like Pilobolus, Mabou Mines, or Frantic Assembly – began as dancers or actors working together as co-artistic directors. As leaders, they created work collaboratively by discussing choices and bouncing ideas off of each other. Together, they forged a distinctive artistic voice that gave their ensemble its identity. With some groups, this turns into rotating projects with one person directing a specific project (e.g., this piece is Ruth's project while this next one is Lee's). Not everyone is in every piece, and these groups often become incubators for a range of projects that still fit within the established aesthetic of the "parent" company, sometimes going off into new areas. As individual artists develop their own voices, they sometimes leave and form a new group or solo career. Steven Hoggett left Frantic Assembly to work on other productions. Moses Pendelton left Pilobolus to form Momix, while Martha Clarke left to develop her own dance/theater pieces like *Vienna Lusthaus* and *The Garden of Earthly Delights*.

A prime example of the co-director structure is *Blue Man Group*, led tightly by the three original Blue Men who created the company and developed the look, philosophy, and material that now has dozens of Blue Men performing in theaters around the world. So precise in their vision is the casting that you must be the same height more or less as the original member of the company you are auditioning for, and the personality types are cloned, literally, in performance so that the same dynamic created by the hugely successful originals is duplicated. Few ensembles have chosen to so carefully "franchise" their success. You can think of it as excellent quality control, or a way of working for a benign dictatorship: I suspect it is a bit of both, giving actors a chance to be in this remarkable show and see the world through Blue Men's eyes. But basically, all of the creative choices have been made for you before you enter the rehearsal hall.

Similarly, the Swiss troupe *Mummenschanz* was co-directed by its three founding members. Several actors have since replaced members during long runs on Broadway and on tour, but like Blue Man, all the creative choices had been made and actors are hired to reproduce those choices night after night. I think the real excitement as a devising ensemble belonged to Andre, Floriana, and Bernie, the original troupe who met as students at Lecoq's school and created a show that became a worldwide phenomenon.

Controlled chaos

This is not a model I recommend you employ full-time, but it does have real value. Regardless of the ensemble model you employ, there is one commonality to almost every creative group I know that should be embraced. Chaos. It is a necessary part of the creative process. Every group should allow for some divine chaos time. It's disturbing to be around, but there is a huge payoff to allowing vigorous brainstorming to take place for extended periods of time in rehearsal. Allow the intuitive side of the brain to rule once in a while, and have a system in place for focusing the energy when you need to call things to order. The best nuggets of inspired performance grow out of a state of controlled chaos and creative freedom. The skill comes in being able to capture the inspired moments from free play and to mine them for use in the context of a show. This is when you need to switch gears and work the left side of the brain: when the room gets quiet, focused, and precise. This is when the teacher, director, or leadership system needs to step up and say, "time to focus". You can do this by taking notes right after a vigorous creative session and asking everyone to jot down details in writing, or recording the whole event on video and wading through it later to look for gold.

The hard work of polishing, analyzing, and re-playing those moments is often the secret behind a piece's success. Each moment, each action, and each word must be mapped out methodically. This calls for a complete change in tone and seriousness of purpose as you make decisions using repetition (the French word for rehearsal) rather than inspiration. Edit what was said or done by people who were just playing around wildly a few minutes ago, and turn it into something intentional. You need actors who are willing to do both. And work outside the rehearsal hall counts as well. I once saw a wildly creative Japanese dance/theater troupe called *The Condors* and took a workshop with them. When asked where their ideas came from, they said from drinking and talking together a lot. At first I thought they were being ironic, but it turns out that really is an important part of their process. Many great ideas get tossed around over dinner, at a bar, or in a hotel or van while touring a show. This should be considered a part of the process as well.

Pick-up groups

Some artists come into a town with a plan, audition local people or have them sign up for a workshop, and then develop material with this new local group using an established model they bring into the community, sometimes weaving local people into an existing piece with other permanent company members. The dancer Bill T. Jones led a community residency to teach local people to be performers in his piece *Still/Here* in every city he presented the work. The Cornerstone Theater Company[3] of Los Angeles built its reputation on community engagement and lengthy residencies working with local people to develop an original production based on community issues. Theater for Social Justice activist Norma Bowles goes into a community and works with groups of people for anywhere from three hours to three months to shape a piece which the participants perform. Sometimes this work relies on collaborative decision making, sometimes on an artistic director making decisions, but the idea that ensemble can be a temporary and valuable experience for an assorted group of people who may never work together again is a model worth mentioning.

Passing the baton

Many groups have survived the transition from original members leaving, founders dying, and real-estate challenges by passing the baton to new people. Groups may re-form with new members, or new groups may inherit the artistic homes of groups that disband. Aspiring artists with fresh energy often pick up where previous groups left off, maintaining the investment in sweat equity and building on the foundation left behind by others. It may take one group ten years to build a center, an audience, and an identity. A new group may inherit that space or name and in their first year get more done in a shorter period of time by building on the shoulders of those who came before. So if your group forms and fades away, take comfort in knowing you may contribute to a chain of events that help future generations. If you have been renting a space, see if you can find a like-minded ensemble to take over the lease. The small-theater that Beau Jest ran for years in Boston began as a boiler room in the back of an old piano factory. Over the years it became a dance studio, an experimental art collective, a rehearsal space, and a theater rental hall that was recently forced to close to make way for a fitness center. But hopefully somewhere a non-profit is cleaning floors and walls and getting ready to open a new performance space that will become home to more ensembles that pass it forward for decades to come.

Owning the space

In Chicago, a successful organizational model is The Steppenwolf Theater, which began as a small collective working out of a church and a school basement, and now has built and owns its own arts complex. The center has spawned more experimental work, as well as restaurants, cafes, and nightlife nearby. They now produce Tony Award-winning work that transfers to Broadway (*August: Osage County*, *Grapes of Wrath*) while still maintaining a core company that includes founding members. Although few ensembles have the resources to own real estate and manage a space, finding a secure place to work is key for any group in the long run. Ellen Stewart made the La Mama Theater complex in New York a home for countless ensembles because of her commitment to fostering work and her visionary development of the fabulous theater spaces she helped own and occupy. Partnering with established groups, colleges, and other non-profits to share or rent space will help to guarantee that your group can continue to make work.

6 *Full-Length Pieces*

Introduction

Full-length pieces are deeply satisfying to work on and incredibly complicated to make. This chapter addresses these larger, more complex challenges, and as a result is more narrative in approach and less a series of exercises. I have attempted to point out some of the differences you will find when working with each source, and tactics for starting out. The sources described here are used frequently for devising full-length works. I only discuss sources I have had direct devising experience with: there are many others. I begin with production issues universal to all devising sources for full-length shows, then talk about each source separately in more detail with specific tactical suggestions. You may be using a source other than those covered in this book, such as Documentary Theater or Immersive Theater, but many of the ideas in this chapter will still apply.

Full-length pieces at their core grow out of a Big Idea that unifies the piece. Finding this start point requires more thought than the prompts described thus far. Your ensemble needs to decide what you want to say, what issue you want to explore, what world you want to create. This almost needs to come before you settle on which film, novel, event, or original idea will best serve your purpose. My company has at times gone into a project on a hunch, and defined the spine as we went along – but that means being comfortable with a high degree of uncertainty in the process. Once you agree on a direction and chose a source or sources to work with, it is time to devise your approach.

Some devising ensembles use new collaborators on each project and create shows with different aesthetic looks and feels to them. Some use the same core group and do shows that have a recognizable aesthetic from show to show while the subject matter changes. Some ensembles work exclusively within a specific expressive form such as shadow theater, mixed media, musicals, or a clown or drag sensibility. Whatever path you take, full-length shows have a longer narrative arc to fulfill than any of the prompts described earlier in this book. They need more rehearsal, more feedback, more self-examination, more discussion, more outside eyes, and more collaboration with a larger circle of technicians, artists, and production people. The risks are bigger, and so are the rewards. Using any of these sources as the basis for a full-length piece deserves a book of its own, so my comments here are modest, meant simply to point you towards a few possibilities. If you are working with classmates in a college setting, you will need at least a semester, if not two, to take on a project of this scope.

The content of your show will be dictated by who leads your rehearsals. Who decides what to work on each day? Is there a writer in the company or artistic directors who shape the piece before it goes to the company? Do you spend time experimenting with themes before narrowing down your selections? Who has final say over the piece? How do you handle the editing choices? Do you need a co-director? Do designers give feedback in rehearsals and help determine what goes in? Or do they do the design work before rehearsals begin? These core aesthetic and logistical questions will affect production choices as much as the source material itself, if not more so.

Time frames

Time frames for work vary wildly. Beau Jest typically spends a year or two on one project. Some companies use much shorter time frames. London's Frantic Assembly and Chicago's Lookingglass Theater can build a piece over a four- to five-week period (with substantial pre-planning). There is no ideal length. Your time frame may be long or short, driven by circumstance or company work patterns. It should be based on how quickly your group makes decisions, how much you want to experiment, and how much time you need as a group to do any deep thinking. It may also be affected by space and personnel availability. Whatever sources you choose to work with, the time frame is one of the main elements dictating the devising process that you do have control over from the beginning. Once you have made a full-length show or two, you will be better able to estimate as an ensemble the time frame needed for a particular project.

Even with a clear idea and time frame going into a piece, the nature of each source presents different challenges. When my company adapted a film, *The Seven Samurai*, we had a strong spine and a six-month timetable. But early attempts to capture some of the dialogue in the film and the emotional content of the story were

Figure 6.1: Samurai 7.0, *Beau Jest Moving Theatre (Lisa Tucker, Larry Coen, Robert Deveau, Jordan Harrison, Elyse Garfinkel, and Scott Raker), Calderwood Pavilion, Boston, MA, 2007. Photo: Justin Knight*

comic and foolhardy, and we had to shift course when handling scene work. It took several weeks of brainstorming before arriving at an appropriate mix of movement, language, and visual projections to meet our initial goals. We did not know we would have that problem when we began, but we knew we had enough time to solve it, and did several experiments before settling on a preferred method (Figure 6.1).

When we adapted a comic strip, *Krazy Kat*, the process was reversed. We knew Herriman's language would work perfectly on the stage, but translating the static, two-dimensional characters into moving, three-dimensional human beings (or puppets) took a period of months to arrive at solutions. Fortunately, we had given ourselves a year to make the piece. So leave some room in your time frame planning for the unexpected, and know that once the theater is booked, all things work backwards from that point. You can only make the show that your time allows, so budget for the time you need upfront.

Make a calendar

Action
Choose the material you want to work with, then look at the calendar. Develop your time frame for research, rehearsal, and presentation. When is the best time to present your work? How often can you meet with your collaborators? What space is available to

work in? What time constraints do you want to put on the project? What time constraints do outside events put on you? How can you muster the time and materials needed to do justice to the theme/story/source you are pursuing? Include in your planning how ideas will be negotiated, and who will have final say on any conflicts. Allow some "wiggle" room for the unexpected to happen, what budget planners would call "contingency". Give yourselves the time you need to fully realize your ambitions.

Making decisions

With ensemble devising, hard questions about structure, arc, the world you are in, the way characters are portrayed, and the story you want to tell will surface at every turn. On any full-length piece, you must find a way to make choices. Democratic muddling through can work in small bursts, but it usually can't sustain the development of a full-length piece. The efficiency with which you make decisions and the comfort level all collaborators have with buying into that structure will determine how long and how painful your rehearsal process will be. Even the most successful devising ensembles will experience vertigo and feelings of doubt when faced with choices, so a process needs to be in place for negotiating solutions. Be clear as a group how the deep thinking for the show will be guided. Is there one director? One writer? A group vote? Rotating roles? Weekly planning sessions? Someone must say, "let's work on this today", "let's go this way", and "time to stop experimenting". I will assume if you are reading this chapter you have found a way to make decisions. If not, read the previous chapter on common decision-making models. Someone needs to decide what world you are in, what questions you are pursuing, what materials you are using, and how it will be expressed on stage. These deeper questions can take weeks or months to determine collectively, or you can delegate them to a person or persons. If your ensemble clarifies these questions early on, you will be able to rehearse using a much shorter time frame.

Clear the air

What is your organizational structure? How does your ensemble create?

Action
Discuss how your ensemble makes decisions. Make sure every voice is heard. Who decides what project is next? Who sets the agenda for rehearsals? When are design ideas discussed? You may want an outside person to facilitate this discussion, as it may be difficult for people to speak honestly. Is there a long-range plan for your group?

Are you just thinking from project to project? Where would you like to be as a group two years from now? Can debate and contrasting ideas help to make better work? Do people want to re-structure how decisions are made in the group, or work with guest directors or designers? Is your work funded? Who provides the funding? Who did the work of getting the funding? It helps to clarify work roles and future plans so that no one person burns out or harbors resentments, and the ensemble can work to its best potential.

Focusing the work

Somehow, either from an individual or a strong creative team, your full-length work needs a focus, a question that drives all decisions. A spine is needed for any full-length piece, and a guiding intelligence is needed to sharpen the focus of the work and structure the rehearsal process. This can be very difficult to do if the director or directors are also performers in the piece. Typically, they need to take a smaller role in the piece or sit it out so that they can maintain some objectivity and see the work as a whole from "outside". At the Intersections Symposium sponsored by the Network of Ensemble Theaters in New York in November 2014, the legendary actress from the Living Theater, Judith Malina, explained the process that director Erwin Piscator used with members of the Dramatic Workshop. They talked for days, weeks, or longer about what they *wanted to say first*. Once they knew that, they would then choose which play to work on.

Define the spine

Action

Choose a project, and discuss as a group what your spine is. Why are you all excited about working on it? Examine the spine regularly. You might discover a new spine halfway through rehearsals that feels more important than your original inspiration. State it and restate it as your rehearsals move towards performance, and let it fuel your work. Adherence to the spine dictates whether to add a dance, cut a monologue, make a new scene, or examine something from a wholly different perspective. For example, the spine for Spymonkey's production of *Oedipussy*, after the initial excitement of deciding as clowns to do a Greek Tragedy, was the theme of "time passing". In a video the company put out on their devising process with director Emma Rice, the actors explained that the personal theme of actors aging and their reaction to a negative review in Edinburgh on their last show helped drive their work on the piece, as well as the impulse to mash up Oedipus with a 1960s sci-fi *Barbarella* aesthetic.

Big Ideas and framing devices

Before you begin rehearsals, also explore Big Ideas and framing devices (which will affect your casting).

Action

Get everyone together to discuss images, sensual landscapes, brainstorms, and themes within the source. What do you see on stage? What matters to you in the story? Why do this project now? What is it really about? Is there one Big Idea or framing device that will guide your production and serve the spine? Make a list of the most far-fetched possibilities. Test out cheaply anything you can, using prototypes or rehearsal props before committing to a Big Idea. Out of this process, the look and feel of the show will emerge and the framing lens will give structure to your rehearsals.

We often have a Big Idea meeting with the cast and designers a couple of months before rehearsals begin to iron out who is human and who isn't, and what the general frame for the playing area will be. Lee Breuer's framing device for *Dollhouse* was that all the men would be little people, and all the women tall. This then had a ripple effect on all design and casting choices. Philadelphia's Pig Iron Theater set *Measure for Measure* in a modern-day morgue. Such radical reframings demonstrate the boundless opportunities available to any devising ensemble when they scratch below the surface of a source.

Variations

Some companies choose early on to create a world inspired by a specific painter or painting. Some groups involve live music and a specific composer or musician at the outset. Some devised projects are made possible because of unique, one-time collaborative opportunities. Canadian director Robert Lepage and his company Ex Machina did *The Tempest* wanting to see what could be done with typical rehearsal room chairs and tables. The American performer Fred Curchack did *The Tempest* as a solo show with a cigarette lighter and a shadow screen. Canadian Susannah Hammnett did *King Lear* as a solo clown show through the lens of a female fool, Norris. Behind all these production's frames is the elusive "why?" What inspired these artists to create these specific worlds? What Big Ideas or framing devices excite your ensemble?

Casting

The casting decisions in an ensemble are often the reverse of the normal casting process. You already have the actors, so you need to decide which roles they will play, and whether you need to add or subtract any actors to the ensemble. In Beau Jest we do this collaboratively, with all the actors in the room together trying out different parts. This process can take a day or a couple of weeks. If some of the characters are masks or puppets or video projections, make those decisions early, before rehearsals begin. Constructing masks and puppets takes time and actors need time to work with them. Video designers need time to shoot and edit. The beauty of masks or puppets is that different actors can play the same role and not confuse the audience, so you can still make casting changes after rehearsals have begun. Video is less forgiving, and must match up concept and execution early on so that what is shot and projected uses the correct actors, background, etc. Masks, puppets, and video do give you the added ability to make quick transitions from one scene to the next.

Pitfalls

Trickier politically is telling people who have worked on previous shows that there is no role for them in the current production. Choices for a framing device will impact casting and other choices. That needs to be determined before everyone in the company gets too excited about being in the next project. Once you decide as a group or as the director what is needed, the company can determine whether they have a member able to play the part, or whether they need to find someone new for the role. One solution is to invite company members to be part of the creative process in another way: as dramaturgs, outside eyes, help with marketing, design, production, and so on. There are many roles to fill in any project; not everyone needs to be in every show. It's good to ask people you've worked with whether they would like to be involved in other ways if their traditional role is not needed.

Getting specific

Action
Study your source for central design images, and find the two to three most essential elements needed for the theatrical world. Purchase some rehearsal props or materials, and start experimenting with design concepts to make sure they work for all scenes.

When we did *Ubu Roi*, we felt that it was a satiric play about the abuse of power, full of battle scenes and multiple murders. There were five actors in my company, so we first decided who played what parts. Our co-director was a puppet and mask designer who helped us decide who was human, who was masked, and who was a puppet. This was also when we looked for musical possibilities so that our composer could write themes and dance music. Besides the five actors and a puppet designer/director we had a composer, a lighting designer, and a set designer. Together we developed the concept of the show, which was based on potatoes, burlap, and wooden poles.

Prototypes

Action

Test out Big Ideas with cheap prototypes first. If it works, build something permanent for the production.

In *Ubu*, we tried mirrored gloves to see whether they would reflect light onto our eyes when we mimed opening a treasure chest (it worked, didn't need to buy a chest). Instead of a campfire, we tried a rippling light effect (less effective, had to build a prop campfire). When Ubu became king and addressed a crowd, we wanted to use rakes as hands to create the image of cheering masses (worked, but needed to add giant paper maché backings to the rakes to make it effective). Knowing that a table was needed, we figured out how many ways it could be used before building it. We ended up with a unit that was a table on one side, a staircase on another, and a rocking see-saw on its third face. We knew early on that the scene where Ubu interrogates and slaughters all of the nobles had to be done as a Punch and Judy show, so a booth was built into the design of the set and wooden puppets were carved that could handle severe batterings (Figure 6.2).

Objects/props

Many shows have iconic objects or props that become central to the work. I recommend finding the materials you want to use early on so that actors have plenty of time to work with them and invent. In Beau Jest shows, *Krazy Kat* had bricks, *Samurai 7.0* had grass fronds and bamboo, *Ten Blocks on the Camino Real* used skeletons (Figure 6.3).

Director/designer Julie Taymor uses the term ideograph[1] to describe objects or images central to the design of a show. In *The Lion King*, it was the image of a circle. Puppeteer Paul Zaloom likes objects that have a double meaning, so he will use a corkscrew in his table-top theater to play a cop, pencils to be students, or herd a pile of cotton balls as sheep.

Action

Look through the script, story, book, or film for a key mood, image, line of dialogue, or metaphor that will guide what objects and props to bring to rehearsal. They may not all end up in the show, but they usually lead to positive next steps that give you something concrete to work on as you move from abstract ideas to reality on stage. Do

Figure 6.2: Ubu Roi, *Beau Jest Moving Theatre (Elyse Garfinkel, Lisa Tucker, Chris Wilder, Karen Tarjan, and Davis Robinson), Boston Center for the Arts, Boston, MA, 1988. Photo: Roger Ide*

Figure 6.3: Krazy Kat, *Beau Jest Moving Theatre (Larry Coen and Lisa Tucker), The Lyric Stage, Boston, MA, 1996. Photo: Bill O'Connell*

scene study rehearsals with props or objects nearby in case an idea strikes.

With *Ubu Roi*, we spent two months working with one prop: three-foot long wooden poles, which became the primary story-telling device for our show. We wanted poles because they were a natural material and they could be used as tools, abstract shapes, or weapons for military drills and battle scenes. We wanted natural materials because it seemed appropriate to the primitive spirit of *Ubu*. The set and costumes were all influenced by wood and burlap. We tied giant burlap potatoes to the poles and invented our own battering rams. We found an acrylic dowel that shone like a light sabre for Bougerlas, the hero of the play. We developed a production number with poles. We created the ship Ubu escapes on in the finale. The more we solved by manipulating the poles, the less we needed to build out the set. I am a big believer in using everything that is on stage in a show, and if possible, using it multiple ways.

Finding a calling

Sometimes, your work will be driven by a strong sense of mission. Our involvement with two un-produced plays by Tennessee Williams led us directly to two projects: *The Remarkable Rooming House of Madame Le Monde* and *Ten Blocks on the Camino Real*. Our mission was a desire to contribute to the theater community's current re-evaluation of Tennessee's lesser-known or neglected works. Moises Kaufman and the Tectonic Theater were on a mission when they went to Laramie, Wyoming, and interviewed people for the play that would eventually become *The Laramie Project*.

Action

Is there a strong social, cultural, or artistic question you are all burning to pursue? If not, perhaps it isn't the right time for your company to make a new piece. Keep searching for the topic that fires up everyone's imagination, that has a momentum pulling others along with you.

Ten Blocks on the Camino Real is the original one-act version of the three-act play *Camino Real*. It was written in 1946, between *The Glass Menagerie* and *A Streetcar Named Desire*. It is a treasure trove of imagery. This was an important piece of theater for Tennessee that we felt was overlooked and under-sung. Some scholars see a clear change in the tone of Tennessee's writing from his earlier, more sympathetic characters, to the more bitter self-absorption of some of his later creations. According to his friend Donald Windham, the change in tone happened between the early version of *Ten Blocks* and the later three-act version of *Camino Real*. We felt it was important to capture as much as possible the beauty, the music, and the magical hallucinations of a delirious traveler looking out a train window as he passed through remote Mexican villages and day-dreamed, fearing he might be dying on a journey following the loss of a lover and in need of spiritual solace.

Our spine became a quote from TW: "If you dissolve the shimmer of mystery over this thing, you lose its fascination". He wanted to put on stage what painters like Picasso had done in the art world. He wanted Giorgio de Chirico, dances, music, and a surreal, dream-like quality using the stage as a three-dimensional poetic canvas, not a conventional three-act plot with symbols explained away. This became our mission as well, and we were happy to spend a year and substantial resources to make it come true for Mr. Williams.
We worked on that show with a constant sense of him being over our shoulders, hoping he would be pleasantly surprised by the results.

Back burners

No piece can be all things to all people, so save some ideas for other pieces. Focus on being true to your source material. If someone makes an offer, you try it, and if it doesn't fit, put it on the back burner for future projects. If it is important, it will surface again elsewhere.
My general rule of thumb is that if after three tries an idea doesn't work – if you keep trying to make a square peg fit a round hole – stop forcing it. Move it to the back burner and use it later or let it fade. Even with a source as tangible as a script, novel, or film, the variety of ways your group can confuse the story by being too in love with a clever idea is infinite. Try to sense when you are forcing, and let it go.

Now let's look at each source in more detail.

Sources: Scripts

Scripts are an obvious choice for full-length pieces. The roadmap is already laid out and your group can spend most of its time on how to tell the story, not what is the story. What is not so obvious when working with a script is how many directions you can go once you begin thinking outside the box. How much input do the actors and designers have in the story? Are you working with a director, with a framing device, with a Big Idea? How does an ensemble approach a script differently than the traditional process of producer, playwright, designers, director, and actors?

First of all, ensembles choose a script that is right for them – that meets their mission and the artistic desires of all the people involved in the project. In traditional repertory theaters the season is chosen by the producers or artistic director and then designers, actors, and directors are jobbed in for the project. With ensembles, that process is reversed. The cast/company exists; finding the right script comes next.

Choosing a script

Scripts that lend themselves well to an ensemble approach are ones in which the playwright invites open-ended solutions to problems with possibilities for masks, improvisation, puppetry, object manipulation, dance sequences, added music, scenic and textual mash-ups or collages, video design, and creative casting. A play like *Ubu Roi* meets all those requirements, which is why my company chose it as our first full-length piece. Jarry gives no explanation for how to go from Poland to Russia, from cave to countryside, or how to stage the various murders and chase scenes. Our company had five actors at the time, so part of the creative excitement for Beau Jest was figuring out how to stage crowd scenes, battles, and reuse actors in different roles. *Ubu* is also in the public domain, which means there are no royalties to pay and freedom to interpret the text legally. With so many theatrical possibilities, it's easy to see why *Ubu* is often a source for ensemble devising. The mother lode, of course, in terms of possibility and free rein is Shakespeare and the Greeks. Ensembles around the world return to these sources every year.

Action

Find a script that excites your ensemble. Examine your shared principles. Are you interested in gender identity? Heightened language? Power struggles? Drag camp? Object theater? English folk songs? A social/political issue? A time period? Then ask yourselves whether the script lends itself well to an ensemble approach.

Pitfalls

Some scripts resist bold interpretations by an ensemble, and should be performed pretty much as written. *Waiting for Godot* is a brilliant script, but it requires actors and directors to faithfully follow the stage directions and text as written. It does not leave a lot of room for devisers to experiment with. Designers have sometimes taken liberties (at their peril) with changes to the locations specified by Beckett, but the estate will not approve language changes or gender switches counter to Beckett's intentions. Beckett himself famously tried to shut down director Joanne Akalaitis's production of *Endgame* when she shifted the location of a bare room with two windows to an abandoned underground subway platform. The Beckett estate is open to new ideas and has allowed a post-hurricane Katrina *Godot* set in New Orleans. Puppeteers and video designers have been given permission to interpret some of his plays, but usually within a strict set of guidelines. If your group is hungering to put its own stamp on a work, I recommend you start with a different kind of play. Read several, and report back to the ensemble with the ones that excite you most.

There are modern playwrights whose works are copyright protected who invite ensemble solutions to imagery and acting challenges. Ionesco, Suzan Lori Parks, and Charles Mee, to name a few, do not always spell out how they want their work performed. Lorca's impossible plays and Tennessee Williams' experimental plays leave lots of room for exploration. Sarah Kane's *Psychosis 4:48* is all language with no designated speakers. From Sophocles to Sondheim, devising ensembles have found numerous ways to approach plays with fresh ideas while still remaining true to the author's intent and language. And some artists intentionally explode the author's intent or stretch it beyond recognition into a wholly new work, at which point the ensemble may need to re-name the work as an original piece to avoid issues of copyright infringement. Follow the path that most excites your ensemble.

Copyright law

A word about *copyright law*. If you are doing a play written within the last 75 years, it is probably still under copyright protection. Permission must be granted to perform it, and a royalty must be paid. Any changes to the setting, the writing, the characters, or the stage directions must be granted in writing. Some estates, such as Samuel Beckett's, and some living playwrights, such as Edward Albee, are very diligent about seeing that the intentions of the writer are honored when the work is licensed. So make sure you are either working with material in the public domain, have permission for your interpretation, or are creating a wholly new work of art under the Fair Use or satire clause of copyright law (a murky area to define) with its own distinct title and authorship. This is the clause that Ryan Landry, the writer/actor/leader of the Gold Dust Orphans[2] troupe in Boston, has exploited liberally in his original shows that play off of classic texts and films with titles like *Phantom of the Oprah*, *The Plexi-glass Menagerie*, *Silent Night of the Lambs*, or *Pussy on the House*.

First steps

Action
Once you have chosen a play, read the script out loud as a group. What exciting possibilities do you envision? In this first phase, it is really useful to have all of your collaborators in the room: designers, musicians, anyone you think might be involved in the production.

Once you have chosen a play, the research and brainstorming begins. Notate all the early ideas. They are often the most imaginative and exciting. All of them hold budget and personnel implications, but if you can get half of them into your final production, you'll be doing well. Many of these early ideas can be accomplished on a tight budget if you persevere and commit the elbow grease to doing the work. Assign homework for everyone and decide how far afield you would like your initial research to go. Once primary and secondary sources have been pursued, collected and presented back to the group, you are ready to focus the devising process on solving the Big Ideas and putting the piece together.

Pitfalls

I think it is worth saying at this point that sometimes script choices that initially excite can fall flat after the research phase. If the group finds the energy level and interest fading instead of growing, change horses now. As infuriating as working on a show can be, the group should feel more pulled and inspired in its march towards completion than fatigued. Beau Jest was once interested in an unknown script, but chose instead to do Aristophanes' *The Birds* because it seemed a safer bet. After spending a couple months working on it, we realized we didn't really have a compelling reason to do it. We recognized that our hearts weren't in it, and as doubtful as we were about the original idea, we went back to the unknown script and had a much more fulfilling time working on it. There was nothing inherently wrong with choosing *The Birds*, but it wasn't the right project for us at that time, and it took us a while to recognize that. A necessary detour.

Content

What is a play script? It is a series of stage directions and words on a page meant to be spoken out loud. That is the primary source – the original text and all its draft versions or translations. Secondary sources that come into play when devising with a script may include the life of the author, letters, critical responses to the play, historical events referenced in the play, issues or events contemporaneous to when the play was written or set, and the lives of the participants in their journey making the piece, including random events and personal incidents that occur while rehearsing. If you choose to set the play in a different location or time period, then that is added to your research as well. A third layer of sourcing is the intentional mash-up of unrelated scripts, music, or design elements that excite the imagination, such as Punchdrunk Theater's decision to mash-up *Macbeth* with Hitchcock's film of the novel *Rebecca* in *Sleep No More* and use Bernard Herrmann film music to tie it together and trigger the actions of the performers.

Interpretation

My college directing teacher would say, "If you can find it in the text" then it is justified. A close reading of the script will lead to wise choices. The Bristol Old Vic/Handspring's *Midsummer* made a brilliant choice for the portrayal of Bottom, as rooted in the literal and obvious meaning of the word Bottom as could ever be imagined. It was jaw-droppingly good. I never realized how often the word "wood" was mentioned in *Midsummer* until after seeing their production, which used a lot of natural wood elements in the set design and the action of the actors and the puppets.

Visionary directors like Lee Breuer of Mabou Mines and Sean Graney of The Hypocrites have given traditional plays by Henrik Ibsen (*Dollhouse*), Gilbert and Sullivan (*Pirates of Penzance*), and J.M. Barrie (*Peter and Wendy*) some very original interpretations. These are director-driven pieces born out of the fervid imagination of the artists, developed with company members, and the resulting shows have all the hallmarks of a bold and committed ensemble in performance. The Fiasco Theater, a small group of musically talented actors who met at Brown University, found great success in New York doing a stripped down, five-person musical version of *Cymbeline*, and have since applied the same ensemble approach to their productions of *Into the Woods* and *Measure for Measure*. Companies across the globe have found numerous ways to interpret scripts. While many of these works are director driven, several also benefit from the process of devising, especially in the early stages of their development and in their fine-tuning.

A new work can take over your life. Every time you are at a bus stop, riding a train, shopping, or taking a shower, you begin to see the world through the lens of the play you are working on. Brainstorms will occur if you keep searching, keep asking. The most random thing heard on the radio may be just the trigger you need to make an inspired choice for the piece you are working on. But it isn't just fate or an accident. You are living your life with every pore open to possibility and every critical cell in your brain tuned to asking: Why are we making this piece? What is it about? What am I passionate about creating in this world? What is missing from the show? This is a process that is true for all devising projects, not just ones based on scripts.

The world of the play

Every script presents its own challenges. Tennessee Williams' one-acts require very different approaches from battle-heavy *Ubu. The*

Remarkable Rooming House of Madame Le Monde was a play written near the end of Tennessee's life. It took us to the theater archives at Harvard University, which held early drafts and personal notes from Tennessee discussing the play. The grotesque nature of the play with its one claustrophobic location in a London attic seemed to beg the question: Why did he write it?

Action

Let your gut reactions to the play guide your research and interpretive choices. What is the play trying to do? Why did the author write it? What about human nature does it illuminate? How can you frame your discoveries? Is the writing poetic, idiomatic, playful, cruel? As the spine of your approach emerges, let it inform every design, acting, and dramaturgical choice in your production. Every script has its own rabbit hole of choices to go down. The work done on one play will affect your work on the next, but it doesn't make it any easier or provide you with a roadmap you can duplicate. Each show is unique, each show is difficult, and each show will dictate its own process and rewards.

Tennessee's sense of betrayal by close friends fueled his writing of *Madame Le Monde*, so letters from that period were an important source. His own failing health and sense of being cut off from everything and everyone led to the central image of a man with crippled legs living alone in an attic and getting around by swinging on hooks. Understanding Tennessee's impish sense of humor and recurring archetypes came from reading his other plays and several biographies. Speaking with Tennessee's secretary from the time the play was written in the early 1980s was invaluable and helped to frame our Big Ideas for the show. Given circumstances also dictated our early choices.

Imposing limits

Action

Clarify the limitations affecting your production. Make a list and keep it nearby so you can make sure you are not caught later on by unforeseen but avoidable conflicts.

For *Madame Le Monde*, the limits were:

- The estate gave us permission as long as we followed all the stage directions and used every word as written.
- The set had to be built to tour, as it was commissioned in two different theaters.
- We wanted real metal hooks hanging from the ceiling that a person could swing on.

- We needed a costume design that "created" the cripple's body, while leaving the actor free to move.
- Grotesque actions would be played in British Music Hall style.
- A sense of poetry and longing were needed for the finale to redeem the mayhem.
- A shadow screen masking violent sexual acts had to be visible in some form to the audience, as the acts were meant to be both a painful and humorous entrance into the main character's world.
- Tennessee's wicked sense of humor and his interest in juxtaposing tenderness with cruelty were key to staging the play.

American Gothic, a much earlier piece written when Tennessee had just graduated from college while in the thrall of gangster movies, poetry, and Midwest Americana, asked for the creation of a very different world with its own set of limits. The performance was outdoors and site specific, on the front porch of a house meant to resemble the iconic setting of the Grant Wood painting. Unlike the psychological journey of *Rooming House*, *American Gothic* was fueled by paintings, blues music, gangster dialogue, and performing outdoors in daylight (Figures 6.4 and 6.5).

Action
As you get further into the world of the play you are working on, bring in photos, films, music, literature, anything that seems to touch

Figure 6.4: The Remarkable Rooming House of Madame Le Monde, *Beau Jest Moving Theatre (Jordan Harrison and Larry Coen), Charlestown Working Theater, Charlestown, MA, 2009. Photo: Justin Knight*

Figure 6.5: American Gothic, *Beau Jest Moving Theatre (Lisa Tucker and Davis Robinson), Provincetown, MA, 2010. Photo: Bill O'Connell*

upon the world of the play you are exploring. The more primary research, the better. Use it all in rehearsal.

No compromises

Action
When you are working on a project, decide what you will not compromise on. What *must* you have in the show, and how will you get it? No matter how much work it takes, do it.

For us with *Ten Blocks*, that meant early on knowing:

- The first peasant killed in the square had to be an inhumanely wizened old puppet.
- The street sweepers had to be malicious and frightening masks.
- The music had to be lively and haunting, with a live band.
- We needed a composer to create customized tonal soundscapes.
- We had to do a skeleton dance homage to cartoon animator Ub Iwerks.
- Don Quixote had to be noble and ridiculous.
- The set had to swirl and dissolve as easily as did the images in the play.
- Kilroy had to be an all-American stereotype of a big, handsome GI.
- The gypsy's daughter had to be sexy and dangerous.
- The monologues needed to have live music like beat poetry.

All of these principles were clear to us before we began rehearsing, and all of them found their way into the final show (Figure 6.6).

Stage directions

A close reading of stage directions is critical to staging any play. Scripts often give you permission to add music and dance and do

Figure 6.6: Ten Blocks on the Camino Real, *Beau Jest Moving Theatre (Robert Deveau, Nick Ronan, Robin Smith, Ellen Powers, and Lisa Tucker, musicians Santiago Cardenas and Tamora Gooding), Charlestown Working Theater, Charlestown, MA, 2012. Photo: Stanley Rowin*

your own blocking, but invariably Beau Jest has found points where we had to make a staging decision and weren't sure what to do. Each time, we went back to re-reading the script, the punctuation, and the stage directions, and inevitably we found some clue or key that was hidden in plain sight telling us which way to go, a little gem like a typo that no one had noticed.

I say all of this to point out some ways to approach a script. Is it action-based? Psychological? Stylistic? Design driven? The American director William Ball[3] has a nice rubric for plays using five categories: Language, Character, Psychology, Spectacle, or Idea Plays. When he directs, he looks for what is the dominant element. Usually plays fit one or two of those categories. With Chekhov, character is important; with Shaw, language. With Shakespeare, it is often all five. These dominant elements should affect your choices. If it is an idea play but you focus on spectacle and lose the arguments, you have failed. If it is a character play, but your framing device alienates any sense of character, you have failed. The research, Big Ideas, and framing device for a play need to be driven by the structure, language, meaning, and worldview of the play.

Adaptations: Books, films, comic strips

Novels are similar to plays in that they are both made up of words on a page telling a story. Some novels even contain dialogue. But novels examine the inner lives of characters and describe events with a degree of linguistic detail that does not directly translate to the stage. Staging interiority is a must with novels. Writers are free to tell any story they want without worrying about location shifts or the practicalities of it being staged. It can have a cast of thousands and jump through time and space as the writer chooses. Rules of time, space, and gravity are up to the author. It is an act of pure imagination. Books are read silently by one individual at their own pace, they can be picked up or put down at any time. Not so with theater.

Books vs. scripts

Plays are written to be heard out loud in one continuous flow, on a public stage with a group of people watching and listening. The audience "sees" the story as much as they hear it. For a book to become a play, someone has to decide:

- How do the tools of the stage – actors, sets, lights, costumes, video, music, dance – illuminate certain aspects of the novel?
- What psychological, emotional, thematic, or intellectual concepts in the novel translate into action on stage? When is language the

best tool? Spoken? Recorded? Projected? Danced? How can the "impossible" elements (time shifts, location shifts, tone, inner monologue, literary devices) be translated?

- How much dialogue or language is needed? Do you use any or all of the dialogue in the novel? Do you express any ideas through movement, objects, dance, music? What about exposition or descriptive passages? A novel has no visual elements, just words. Each reader forms their own mental picture of an event. On stage, the devising ensemble does that work for the audience. What physical world best translates the text to the stage, according to your ensemble's aesthetic? And if it *has* illustrations, such as *Wind in the Willows*, *Alice in Wonderland*, or Dr. Seuss books, how will you handle the audience's expectation of that iconographic imagery?

Decisions

Action

Determine how you will answer these big questions. Is there one person in the group who is going to take on the adaptation? A framing device you want to work with? A scene-by-scene approach staying faithful to the book? A radical reinterpretation? One director, or a group effort? Mash-up, clown show, contemporary reimagining?

Literature is a rich source. In this category, I include all forms of writing: short stories, novels, fairy tales, newspapers, diary entries, letters, court transcripts, medical journals, and biographies of authors. They give ensembles a great start in terms of character, narrative, setting, and theme. The variations can be endless, as material is focused through the aesthetic vision of each ensemble. *Moby Dick* was adapted for the stage as a faithful, two-hour meta-drama by Orson Welles using 12 male and 2 female actors. It was also the platform for an inspired clown show by the British troupe Spymonkey as a hilarious four-person version that spends ten minutes on one actor just trying to stand up straight on a slippery deck. The Elevator Repair Service read the entire *Great Gatsby* out loud from cover to cover in an eight-hour production, while New York's Neo-Futurists created a show based on reading the stage directions of Eugene O'Neill's plays out loud while trying to act them out.

Why put novels on stage?

A novel is a private experience where the reader takes in words and builds a mental picture of the events and the inner lives of the characters. The stage is a shared, visual, and aural experience in which you have no choice about how the people on stage sound and act: the whole audience is seeing and hearing the same event and making their own interpretation of what it means. Nuance is still possible, but trying to capture the author's voice by using some kind of narrator, monologue, or recording to paint an inner landscape substituting for the author's voice is often problematic. The inevitable response is "why not just read the book?" You need to make choices about what will work on stage better than on the page. You need to translate the interiority of a novel to the theatricality of the stage.

From what I have seen, the shows that work best translating books to the stage have found a way to plumb the essence of the story, or the audience's expectations of the story, and convert it into a new work of art that can only play on stage. It *has to* exist in the theater's unique medium, and not just serve as a re-creation in three dimensions of the plot and dialogue spelled out in the book. The question to answer is, "I have read the book, why should I see it on stage?" It is the same problem that film producers have when they decide to adapt a play. They are very different mediums. A good stage show needs a strong reason to be made into a film, or it will flop. The same is true of putting a novel on stage. Novels can use pages of description to capture the inner thoughts of the characters. On stage, we can't read what people are thinking, and a whole different set of tools are needed to convey the author's intent through action, dialogue, and design. A musical on stage can use a passionate song to express a character's yearning. In a film, that can be done more effectively sometimes with a five-second close-up.

Need

Action
Discuss as an ensemble why you need to put this novel on stage. What about the medium of theater is better for communicating these ideas or this story? What about your approach makes this a valid theatrical project you are all excited by, that makes you want to spend months devising solutions for?

Which way to go?

The question of whether to do *A Tale of Two Cities* with 20 people and a live orchestra or three people and an accordion is more a result of your given circumstances and desires than it is about the source. *The Hunchback of Notre Dame* was staged by American actors Dan Hurlin and George Sand as a two-person show in the 1980s. They played all the parts using stepladders and swinging light bulbs for a set. So it is not a question of the scale of the source, but of company desires. Who are you? What do you want to do? Why are you attracted to that topic/source? How are you going to use the material? *The Grapes of Wrath* was adapted for the stage by Frank Galati and the Steppenwolf Theater as a period piece with a large cast and strong dramatic roles. Twenty-five years later, Steinbeck's novel was used by Brooklyn-based The Builders Association to draw comparisons between the Dust Bowl and the 2008 mortgage crisis, using footage simulating John Ford's 1940 film of the novel, cross-cut with derivative traders and live video feeds of the actors projected back onto the set in a new piece called *House/Divided*. Both pieces were true to the artistic principles of the companies who made them and, in their own way, to the content of the book.

To bring something to the stage is usually to go down one of two paths: faithful adaptations, or satiric or contemporary reinventions.

Faithful adaptations

Faithful adaptations find a way of suggesting an image or event using all the theatrical tools of space, design, language, and movement to trigger the audience's imagination with a new kind of poetic compression, delighting the audience by letting them see something they were already familiar with from the book, but which uses their imagination to actively participate in a new way of creating that image on stage. This is true whether the source is a familiar novel, film, play, or historic event. Chicago's House Theater did a great job of staging *a Matrix*-style fight scene in *The Curse of the Flying Heart*, using rigging everyone could see, eliciting tremendous applause for one-upping what computer-generated imagery does on screen because it was *real*. There is a similar wave of appreciation in the audience when an iconic passage from a book is brought to life on stage. During the moment from the novel when a starving stranger is breast-fed in a barn by Rose of Sharon in Steppenwolf's production of *The Grapes of Wrath*, you could hear a pin drop. It was a shared, sacred moment of generosity and pain, felt communally and in the theatrical present. The stage is a medium best used for shared, emotional catharsis, for feeling pity, envy, fear, love, anger, or joy when truth is revealed. If your adaptation succeeds, it is usually because you have found a way to put characters on stage that engage an audiences' sympathies, that allows us to identify with their wants and needs and get swept up in the world they are a part of through action, dialogue, and design elements.

In the category of faithful adaptations, there are many examples. The production mentioned above by Steppenwolf of John Steinbeck's novel *The Grapes of Wrath* helped bring the company to national prominence. The Royal Shakespeare Company did an eight-hour version of Charles Dickens' *Nicholas Nickleby* that toured internationally. The musical format is particularly suited to staging novels. Shows like *Les Misérables* or *Matilda* began as novels. These are big-budget shows from mainstream theater that tell their stories using songs, dances, big sets, and a large company of actors. Songs give power and lift to key emotional moments, and the musical theater form allows spectacle and grandeur to transport audiences collectively into the world of the story where normally you would be reading the novel at home alone. This shared, communal uplift is one of the great powers of live theater. I mention these commercial productions because they point to successful models of translation. Devising ensembles can do the same work on a smaller scale, and smart companies like Rachel Dickstein's Ripe Time Theater[4] in New York use sound, language, movement, and design elements to create compelling adaptations of novels on a smaller budget.

Satiric adaptations

The other path ensembles often take is in the world of satire and physical comedy, celebrating the folly of taking on a big story with limited resources. The Reduced Shakespeare Company made a career out of doing every play by Shakespeare in two hours with *The Compleat Works of William Shakespeare (abridged)*. John Barlow adapted the Hitchcock film *The 39 Steps* (itself originally a novel) for the stage using a man, a woman, and two comedians who played all other parts. I have seen a one-man staging of *Don Quixote*. Lifeline Theater in Chicago did *The Lord of the Rings* with tabletops strapped to the backs of actors used as battlefields for plastic action figures. The two actors I mentioned above used stepladders, wine glasses, and a clothesline to create all the imagery in *The Hunchback of Notre Dame*. There are many more examples. This method sometimes evokes more laughter than the original novel intended, but they stand as compelling reimaginings of source material with their own truthful logic and theatrical reality taking us into the world of a novel, perhaps from a lens that hasn't been used before, combining elements that bring new light to the story and the author.

Variations
One other pathway for novels is to transpose the plot structure and characters into a contemporary setting, to make the politics or social issues of that era more relevant to a contemporary audience.

How big?

A big budget and large cast are not often available to most devising ensembles, and it certainly is not a prerequisite for adapting a novel. The two-person *Hunchback of Notre Dame* I mentioned above was very faithful to the novel, with a few nods to the 1939 film as well. Having a stepladder as a spatial metaphor for a cathedral with wine glasses as bells was incredibly effective. Once you realized that two men were going to tell the whole story, you easily became swept up in the way they portrayed Esmerelda, Frolio, Quasimodo, and other characters. The imaginative way in which two actors used simple props and Foley sound effects to create each scene led to a compelling complicity with the audience, and at the same time allowed for the emotional impact of Hugo's story to take hold. It wasn't played for laughs, and the result was a magical, theatrical tour de force.

When Beau Jest adapted H.G. Wells' *War of the Worlds*, we used the original novel, a 1953 film version, the 1978 rock opera with Richard Burton and The Moody Blues, Orson Welle's 1938 panic-triggering radio broadcast, and a devised sequel based on the question, "what would happen if Martians landed in Boston today?" The final show was a bit messy, and a little distance from it makes it pretty easy to see what went wrong. We cast our net too wide. We had too many sources, and didn't do enough to thin our choices down. We probably had enough material for at least two or three shows crammed into the piece, but we presented it as one event. In retrospect, we should have done one piece staying in the 1930s, a second on a dystopian contemporary fantasy of technology run amok, and culled out all references to the Hindenburg disaster and other events that had no bearing on the novel. One of the big dangers with devising is that no one will tell you when to Stop–Stop–Stop. I think it best to err on the side of keeping it simple.

Starting points

Here are a few suggestions for how a theater ensemble can begin devising from a novel.

- Do the paragraph exercise from Chapter 4 using an iconic passage, and see what it triggers. Try a few different versions, and see whether you can begin to zero in on the shape the story telling will take. Are other methods suggested? Try out early on whether you will use a narrator, video projections, puppets, or objects.
- Pursue all research areas the novel triggers. Was it made into a film? How many versions? Are their earlier drafts of the story? What was going on in the author's life when the novel was written? Were there contemporary events that triggered the writing? Was it ever adapted to the stage? How? Why do you want to do it?
- Start defining your spine. Ask yourself again: Why is this novel attractive to us? What do we want to say with it? How do we want to say it?

- Look for objects or materials mentioned in the text that serve as a metaphor for the world of the play. Is there an ideograph to work with, something that is a uniting design principle? Start bringing objects/materials into rehearsal to brainstorm with.
- Try out monologues for different characters. Use actual dialogue from the novel, or improvise off of scenes mentioned or implied in the book. See which characters come to life best.
- Pick out action sequences that look like they might work on stage. Stage them a few different ways. Divide your ensemble into two groups and work in separate rooms on the same problem. Bring the two solutions together and see whether they can be merged, or whether one direction is more fruitful to pursue.
- Look closely at the language of the book for central images, and brainstorm how those can be staged. Is there a Human Truth that can be seen in a different light through a contemporary treatment? *West Side Story* moves Romeo and Juliet's plot to New York City very effectively. Does the novel resonate with a contemporary concern of yours?
- Find a descriptive passage from the novel to use as a choral exercise. Have different members of the ensemble recite it and pass the words around. Can it be turned into an overture? A Dance? A soundtrack to a shadow theater segment?

Staging choices can range from conventional story–theater adaptations to unique solutions like The Elevator Repair Service's brilliant approach to staging F. Scott Fitzgerald's *The Great Gatsby*. Called *Gatz*, the show begins in a run-down warehouse with cluttered shelves and desks. A worker turns his computer on, it won't boot up, so he reaches in a drawer and starts reading the novel. He goes on to read the entire book out loud. The play does a brilliant job of holding our interest for eight hours by creating events in the office on stage that are parallel to the events in the novel. Liquor is taken out of desk drawers and a party unfolds, relationships with co-workers start to mirror events in the novel, and a stage manager sitting at a nearby desk runs music and sound cues throughout the piece to help bring all of the imagery to life. In terms of Big Ideas, I read in an interview that John Collins, the director, likes to use whatever is around when making a show. The rehearsal space they were in when they first began working on *Gatz* was an old warehouse full of clutter, which became the inspiration for the set design of the show.

A good book on the subject of adapting novels for the stage is Vincent Murphy's *Page to Stage*. Be aware that copyright law applies to novels as well as plays, and film companies often tie up a book's rights for years at a time. If the author is still alive, contact them or their representatives to let them know you are interested in doing a stage adaptation of their work, and get permission for the stage rights.

Adaptations: Films

Films present an added challenge to the devising ensemble. In a way, they are a bridge between novels and plays. Like novels, they have storylines and conflicts with richly drawn characters. Unlike novels, films also have visual elements and sound, which create a different set of challenges for devising. Even silent films, which are completely visual, are a treasure trove of information for telling a story. Films can have dance sequences. Films use music. Films have close-ups and a host of cinematic techniques that can be adapted for the stage. But film is a two-dimensional medium played on a large white screen using bright illumination to sweep an audience's eye into a world with its own aural soundscape and visual journey. Film creates an event and projects it in a dark room to transport the viewer into that fabricated world. So there are similarities to theater: both involve audiences sitting together in the dark to go on an imaginary journey. Both rely on a willing suspension of disbelief. But theater is a three-dimensional form happening in real time in the space in front of you; film is a projected, two-dimensional image of another time and place. Films have excellent dramatic dialogue similar to what you would hear on stage, but the mechanics of delivery are different from dialogue spoken on stage, even though many films began as plays.

Film vs. theater

For several reasons, film speaks a language that doesn't translate easily to the stage. Films use shots to establish mood, location, and tempo. Plays use action and set design. Film dialogue and play scripts may look similar on the page, but when you speak film dialogue on stage it has a very different emotional impact than when seen on the screen. Without the close-ups, camera angles, foreground and background framing, music, and cinematography, the magic of the moment on screen requires some real sculpting on stage to be as effective. Film uses realistic settings and special effects that are difficult to create on stage. The meaning of a monologue can be altered in a film by zooming in to a 20 foot-tall detail of the actor's face, or a close-up reaction shot of the person listening. On stage, the audience chooses where to look. In a film, there is less choice. A location shot can move from an interior to an exterior in the blink of an eye, and set up future events or flashbacks using a sophisticated visual vocabulary. Audiences have become accustomed to the narrative tools of cinema – collage, cross-cut, split-screen, fade-out –

and this is both a challenge and an opportunity to exploit for live stage adaptations.

The language of film

Plays share film's ability to use split-screen, collage, flashback, and other narrative devices. Some stage adaptations include video design, creating hybrid performances that are part film, part theater, with actors moving in and out of filmed scenes, tracking performers with live cameras, or using filmed work projected on actors' bodies, props, or the set. One common feature in film is the wide shot, or "establishing" shot.

Action
Pick a film your ensemble is interested in adapting. Choose a wide shot from the film that establishes location, mood, or tempo. Brainstorm ways that your ensemble can create that effect on stage. What scenic elements do you need? How can light and sound help you? What objects or materials will help you create a theatrical equivalent of the same establishing shot? What is the theatrical equivalent of a wide shot?

Variations
Try putting several scenes from the film into a short impression, using the exercise Epic Tales in Short Times found in Chapter 4.

As you dive deeper into the film, many of the same issues found adapting a novel will arise. What characters translate well to the stage? What dialogue? What action? In what form? What aspect of the story interests you most and works on stage? Is there a framing device for your design and casting choices? Filmed performance is the permanent record of a story that remains unchanged whether someone watches or not. In theater, performers are aware of the audience. They are living these events for the audience to experience. If someone laughs or cries in the audience, the alert performer adjusts their timing so that the next line of dialogue can be heard. If a cell phone goes off, someone may stop the play. The scenic expectations are different, and the creative process leading up to the actor's performance is quite different and involves weeks of rehearsal, while a film typically rehearses and shoots an actor's scene on the same day.

Pros and cons

So how would a film classic like *Casablanca* be adapted for the stage? What changes are needed when you transpose it to the medium of live performance? On the easy end of the spectrum, you could find the screenplay and the original play it was based on by Joan Alison called *Everyone Comes to Rick's*. A bar setting is easy to do on stage, and songs like *The Marseillaise* or *As Time Goes By* can be sung live. Memorable roles with an interesting love triangle can work on stage, although creating the ambiance of North Africa during wartime could be trickier. It is worth noting that the film did manage to do this while shooting entirely in Burbank, California, in a fairly artificial way. You may choose to capture some of that Hollywood artifice in your adaptation.

On the challenging end, you are battling preconceptions of how those characters should be played. What you don't have on stage is Humphrey Bogart, Ingrid Bergman, Claude Reins, and a host of memorable character actors who made an indelible impression on how those roles look and sound. You don't have black and white cinematography and close-ups fueled by Max Steiner's melodramatic score to make the drama more visceral. It has become such a favorite for audiences, who are used to hearing those classic lines spoken by those great actors. You are going to need a strong reason for why you should put it on stage. What can you do theatrically that another viewing of the film can't do? What about human nature does the film tap into that theater can shed a new light on? Woody Allen was able to turn his love for the film into another film, *Play It Again, Sam.* If you can answer that question for the stage, you will have a built-in audience of fans of the movie who will flock to the theater to see what you have done with it. That is one of the built-in advantages of doing a show from a well-known novel or film.

Action

Have a brainstorming session with your ensemble, and discuss why the film you want to adapt deserves to be on stage. What would be the theatrical reason? What is the spine of your story going to be? Is there a framing device that would clarify your version? All casting and design ideas will follow out of that discussion.

First steps

If you adapt a well-known film, you must contend with the audience's expectations. There are certain scenes they *must* see, so you need to be aware of that expectation when you work on your version of it. Kurosawa's film *The Seven Samurai* is well known to film buffs, and has some magnificent cinematography and character work we were very conscious of when working on it. We began by making a list of key scenes and iconic moments we knew we had to have in the final piece, and most of them were there or referenced by the time we opened.

Action

Look at the film you want to adapt, and list all the key scenes and visual elements you *have* to put in your adaptation. Check that list against your spine, and make sure you don't spend time working on something extraneous to your concept. Start devising material using all of the prompts found earlier in this chapter, including Objects/Props, Imposing Limits, Prototypes, No Compromises, Faithful vs. Satiric, and Big Idea sessions (Figure 6.7).

Figure 6.7: Samurai 7.0, *Beau Jest Moving Theatre, Boston Center for the Arts, Boston, MA, 2006. Photo: Justin Knight*

Our First Steps adapting *The Seven Samurai* were:

- To experiment with horses. There are lots of horses in the film, from the opening bandit shots and the samurai riding, to the big battle scenes. We tried toy horses, shadow puppetry, and actors as horses with rope harnesses.
- To use grass fronds and curly wood poles to capture images – wind blowing through grain, samurai swords, burial mounds, and peasants hiding from attack.
- To make the village elder a visually compelling, ancient puppet.
- To find passages from Shakespeare describing battle preparations and parallels in the movie to our own folly as actors taking on a massive project (our framing device).
- To decide early on – no Japanese accents and very little dialogue. We selected key scenes and projected titles and dialogue on an overhead screen as supertitles.
- To experiment with staged film techniques including "wipes", split-screen, long shots, soft focus, night shots, changing camera angles, fade-outs, close-ups, and zooms.
- To explore the number seven, and why it is so important.
- To bring in hand fans of all shapes and sizes to use for long shots, close-ups, weapons, symbolic acts, camera angles, and dance sequences.

Choosing a film does not answer what your approach will be. It may even make it harder to answer the deeper question of why do it. Think carefully and creatively about what draws you to the material. Develop a spine and any framing devices. You must then create your own original show, either loosely inspired by or faithfully adapting this film that already exists in another two-dimensional medium. What can you do with it in three dimensions that is worth a year of exploration? You must answer a thousand practical, personal, and philosophical questions for why it belongs on stage, no matter which film you choose. You may first want to decide as a group what driving question your ensemble wants to pursue, and then find a film that will serve those purposes. And don't rule out chance or blind luck. Stephen Sondheim was very interested in looking at the follies of human desire by adapting Jean Renoir's film *The Rules of the Game* while working with the unities of time, place, and action. But he was unable to secure the rights, which led to the search for a film with similar possibilities – Bergman's *Smiles of a Summer Night*, which ultimately became the musical masterpiece *A Little Night Music*. Sometimes, getting turned down can be a good thing.

Adaptations: Comic strips

Many comic strips have been staged successfully, often as musicals. *You're a Good Man Charlie Brown, Doonesbury, Annie,* all started as comics. The freedom in a musical to use the full palette of theatrical tools comes in handy with the often colorful and melodramatic world of a comic. Film seems to be a better vehicle for the action comic strips, such as *Superman* or *The Fantastic Four,* which may in part explain the troubled reception of the recent stage adaptation of *Spiderman, Turn off the Dark.* Green screen technology and computer animation can create images that are much harder to do on stage, so why bother? The huge Dolby sound system of a movie theater can surround the audience with another layer of experience that tends to drown out dialogue, one of the more important tools on stage. The stage is a more humane experience, so comic strips that emphasize character, story, and emotional catharsis of some kind rather than action sequences seem to do better. Even when the characters are bugs, such as the musical *Archy and Mehitabel,* we can enjoy and identify with the results. Recent hit shows like *Astro Boy and the God of Comics* and *She Kills Monsters* have shown that the action/manga genre can also be adapted for the stage. And the Public Theater in New York extended the run of Alison Bechdel's graphic novel *Fun Home,* a musical adaptation by Lisa Kron and Jeanine Tesori, due to popular demand. It is moving to Broadway in spring, 2015. The creative possibilities in a comic strip make them rich territory for ensemble devising.

Key areas to explore with comic strips are:

- Read all the strips, keeping an eye out for recurring characters. Who is most significant, what plot lines keep popping up, and which stories or plots look like they might work well on stage?
- Which of those characters would work better as shadows, videos, puppets, objects, or human actors?
- Look for music opportunities. Are there songs embedded or referenced in the strip? Are there emotional moments or plot points that would benefit from musical treatment?
- What aspects of the strip's material world need to be on stage? Is there an actual material that can be used metaphorically to create the strip's reality on stage? Is it a wood world, a painted world, a projected world, a plastic world, a natural world, a junkyard world? What scenic approach captures the energy of the strip?
- Are there iconic props or objects you can bring into rehearsal for the actors to work with?
- Is there anything in the strip that can be "danced?"

● Look at the use of line in the strip. This can be a source for choreography. What is the rhythm of the line: is it jagged or smooth, fat or fine? Fragmented or bold?

● When the cartoonist implies an action, do the obvious and bring it to life. Try running, walking, crawling, or dancing, using a frame from the strip as a start point. If there are several frames in a row, try moving from one frame to the next as if you were connecting the dots in bring it to life. Pause as you pass through each frame and check the original drawing for accuracy.

● Go round robin with each character, playing with the essential point of view of each character's voice. How would they sound? What are their key expressions? Have different actors give it a shot, and see if you can zero in on what sounds like the authentic voice of the character.

● Contact the cartoonist if they are alive, or the copyright holder of the strip, to see what permission you have to work with the material.

The dance theater company Pilobolus recently collaborated with cartoonist Art Spiegelman, working together in a studio to create a new piece that is now part of their repertoire. Our company was attracted to the world of George Herriman, the cartoonist who created *Krazy Kat*. His drawing was funny, lyrical, magical, absurd, and his story lines were full of existential moments that used a rich invented blend of patois language and Brooklyn-ese that we knew would work well on stage, as well as many silent moments, musical references, and drawn dance numbers that were a joy to put on stage. I am most proud of a scene we invented called "The Little Brick Dance". Following a late-night party where everyone had done the Charleston and passed out, three actors got up, started picking up bricks, looked at each other, and then assembled for a little dance on the floor in the moonlight with the bricks in tribute to Chaplin's dinner roll dance. It was magical, in the world, and yet never drawn in the strip (Figure 6.8).

Historical/current events

A true story or historical event is rich fodder for a full-length piece. Challenges of this source lie somewhere between the constraints of a script or novel and the freewheeling abyss of a completely original show. There may be text or dialogue to draw on, possible threads of a story and some visuals, but the structure is more wide open as a start point. Playwrights are often drawn to this source. *Equus*, *The Maids*, *Evita*, and many other shows are based on real events. I keep a list of possible topics from this source on the back

Figure 6.8: Krazy Kat, *Beau Jest Moving Theatre (Larry Coen, Jay Bragan, and Davis Robinson), Lyric Stage, Boston, MA, 1995. Photo: Bill O'Connell*

burner anytime I hear of a true story that intrigues. For example, Victoria Woodhull, friend of Cornelius Vanderbilt and the first woman Wall Street trader, a free love advocate and presidential candidate, would, I think, make a great piece for the stage someday. Doing something site specific where you live is also a rewarding project. Topics can be found by digging around a town's history, newspaper archives, historical society, or by interviewing people in the community. I've seen excellent student ensemble projects built on a simple local theme, absorbing impressions and then replaying them in a structured order.

Research

Action

Look into the history of your area. Does any story or topic have stage appeal? Is there a major event that tells a bigger tale? A town character or icon? Are there issues in the community your ensemble could address? Is there a closed mill, factory, or business that could serve as the location for a site-specific event? Do you have any "wish list" projects based on true stories or historical events? Spend a few weeks doing research, and see whether it leads you into areas with theatrical potential. Does the energy of the idea peter out as you start looking into it, or does it open up more avenues of investigation? If it peters out, let it drop. If it opens up deeper terrain, then start devising a show. Focus on the theme and decide whether to do a

Figure 6.9: The Cardiff Giant, *Beau Jest Moving Theatre (Lisa Tucker, Lauren Hallal, Patrick Sweetman, Jay Bragan, and Davis Robinson), Tower Auditorium, Boston, MA, 1992. Photo: Teresa Izzo*

literal re-enactment, an exploration of the theme, or a mash-up of several sources from your research. Use some of the other devising exercises in this book to flesh it out further.

Beau Jest became interested in a historical event while working on a piece based on the theme of "Truth and Lies". A friend told us about a true story that happened in 1869 in upstate New York involving a relic called The Cardiff Giant. That story was then used as the main through-line in a piece that also investigated the television quiz show scandals of the 1950s and the Clarence Thomas/Anita Hill Supreme Court nomination battle (Figure 6.9).

The very simple question of "how do you decide who is telling the truth?" became our central theme. Flashes of the television quiz show scandal paralleled the rise-and-fall storyline of both hoaxes. A Hill/Thomas dance and personal monologues about lying were used as "spice" throughout the evening to connect the audience to the performers and the two bigger stories. We also added a section on the body language training politicians are coached in to appear sincere, plus the familiar scene of an eager performer asking his friends post-show what they thought of his performance after what was clearly a terrible show.

The highlight of working on *The Cardiff Giant* was a research road trip the ensemble took to upstate New York to retrace the steps of the original hoax, go to the grave sites of the characters buried in Cardiff, and visit the NY State Historical Society where the actual Cardiff Giant is on display. Primary research can be inspiring. This led to a new sequence about life in upstate NY in the late 1800s. It was an area known then as The Psychic Highway because of the number of strange groups that sprang up in that region: the Oneida Utopian Community who made quality flatware, Joseph Smith who found gold plates that led to the creation of the Mormons, the Fox Sisters who started a nationwide craze holding séances and talking to the dead, the Miller-ites who predicted the date the world would end, and the home of L. Frank Baum, author of the Oz stories. This became part of an opening number, or "establishing shot". The whole trip was photographed and made into a slide show that was used as a coda at the end of the show to "prove" to the audience that it all really happened. Without that road trip, the show would have been half as interesting.

Action

If you are making a piece based on an actual event, make sure there is a contemporary reason you *have* to make the piece. Then:

- Check all primary sources. Visit the source if you can. Read everything written about it. Find people who were there, or wrote about it.
- Interview people connected to the event.
- Investigate parallels in literature, art, or history that speak to the event and its resonance to now.
- Look for musical possibilities. As with novels, there is often music mentioned, or music implied, or music you feel speaks to the issue/event/time of the play you want to make.
- Alternate playing characters to making landscapes to using physical objects. See whether any design ideas start to emerge.
- Is there a painting, film, or visual point of reference that can serve as a tonal key to your work? A composer? Surround the rehearsal room walls with it, dance to it.

Most novels and scripts have a clear beginning, middle, and end that guide the story you are telling. With a historical event, there is more freedom because the event may still be ongoing, or its origins may be shrouded and require invention on your part. The "story" exists in many different versions told from different points of view. My high school history teacher liked to define history as "whoever gets to you the first with the most". So depending on who you talk to and what you believe to be true, you have great freedom to shape the event theatrically to make it the story you want to tell. It may focus on one family, an individual, or cast a wider historical net and examine entire communities or historic trends. No matter how you choose to tell it, I think it will help if you clarify the reason you as an ensemble must tell this story now, and what its focus is before getting too far into working on it.

Atmospheres

Action

Go out as individuals into the town/city you live in, and absorb impressions. Get back together, and make a list of the important spaces and people that define your town. Go back out in pairs or groups and start gathering dialogue, physical impressions, moods, textures, and create short pieces based on the stores, streets, people, and events you observed. Organize that material into a 15–20-minute ensemble impression or collage of the place you live.

This ability to observe and embody for an audience your impressions of a familiar place is a great tool for building an evening-length piece on historical or documentary sources. Lecoq often sent groups from his school out into Paris to observe a specific location and have people come back and stage it for the rest of the workshop as an autocoeur. You can spend a few days on this exercise, or make it part of a larger semester-long project and put in the dramaturgical and rehearsal time needed to make it a full-length piece.

Devising ensembles have presented historic documents as dramatic text, such as reading the transcripts of Oscar Wilde's sodomy trial in Moises Kaufman and the Tectonic Theater's[5] *Gross Indecencies*. There is the documentary theater method of restaging interviews with people affected by a current event, such as Anna Deveare Smith's shows *Twilight* and *Fires in the Mirror*; and groups like The Civilians used interviews, found text and documents on the theme of losing things for their show *Gone Missing*.

Original ideas

Making something from scratch is the essence of devising. It is probably the biggest challenge, which is why I have saved it for last. To make an original piece, realize first that you aren't really starting with nothing. You are starting in this world today, surrounded by images – memories – news – stories – traumas – friends – goals – challenges – fears – hopes – desires. You aren't starting from scratch. You are overflowing with possibilities. The difficulty isn't really thinking of something to work on, it's narrowing down all of the options and picking one for this specific original show.

Topics

Making an original piece requires a theme or topic to drive the creation of the piece. That alone won't solve all your problems; you can choose a good topic and still have a piece that ends up a complete mess, in which case you learn from your mistakes, refocus your idea and make a new piece with the same or a different subject. You can also just give up and go back to working with more structured source material: original work is not for everyone, and there is no shame in abandoning the effort.

But if it interests you, and you have an ensemble excited about making something original, there is nothing like the experience of shared, communal creation. Give it a try: the lessons are invaluable. The well you are all drawing from is quite personal. Exploring your deepest personal images, ideas, and impulses as source material and turning it into material others can connect to is unlike any other creative process for a theater person. One side benefit is that when you go back to working with a traditional script afterwards, it will all seem so much easier.

Action

Gather the people you want to work with and begin training together to develop a shared expressive language through dance, contact improvisation, acrobatics, viewpoints, Lecoq work, singing, clowning, choral harmony, puppetry, or whatever mutual interests bind your group together. Spend at least a month or two developing your ensemble's performance strengths while talking about choosing a start point or theme. Start doing research on that theme, and see whether it leads you to a deeper exploration of the theme or a dead end. Go further with your research and start making material if it is a rich theme. Throw the theme out if it is a dead end and pick a new topic. Adjust the theme or subject over time to keep up with your interests and discoveries. Once it is clear you have found a piece worth pursuing, do all of the exercises outlined at the beginning of this chapter: develop a time line, focus the *spine*, decide on any framing devices, start working with props, objects, and design concepts, and begin the long process of writing, refining, and polishing the work in preparation for its debut.

Pitfalls

If you are doing this work in a school setting as a semester- or year-long project, allow two to three weeks to settle on a topic, with perhaps one week to test the waters and change horses if it doesn't pan out. The rest of your time must be spent rehearsing and fine-tuning the performance. You must lock in a theme within the first month of work and not deviate from it. There is a tendency with young actors to keep debating or being dissatisfied with the direction things are going and wanting to change topics week after week. The group needs to agree on a source for the work and stay with it, and you need rehearsal time, no matter the topic. In fact, the topic is less important than the process of working together, so a teacher or director can save a lot of negotiating time by just saying at the outset that this piece will be based on the theme of _____, and then let them take it from there.

Beau Jest's first full-length original show was called *Motion Sickness*, an examination of the destabilizing nature of change: job changes, leaving home, relationships ending, growing up. We learned a lot about the devising process from working on it. An interesting paradox we noticed was that whether one is moving forward or staying put, both choices can cause nausea. Being trapped by your own inertia is as distressing as destabilizing rapid movements. Motion sickness was a force we swam in for many months, an interesting metaphor for original devising. It took a year to create. The process included hiring our first writer to sit in with us and script some of the dialogue and research the theme. At one point, after a couple of months of drift, we felt completely lost. I seem to recall, in our worst improvised moments, sitting on the floor with a fellow actor trying to invent laws for a foreign country where smoking outside was forbidden and allowed only in jail cells. Clearly, we were floundering in minutiae. Another actress was at the bottom of the sea inside a giant clamshell complaining about the weather and referencing a painting that had no bearing on our theme. Fortunately, our co-director who had been away for a few weeks came in that night, watched us, and said "what are you doing?" Stunned silence. "What is this piece about?" It was a wake-up call. We were shocked and temporarily completely depressed. The company had a total bout of real-time motion sickness, living what had up to that point been mostly an intellectual exercise. We all felt like we had just wasted months of time and needed to throw everything out (Figure 6.10).

Our answer, in desperation, was "it is about the desire to get away from it all". "So do that", she said, and a cloud was lifted. She gave us a major course clarification right when we needed it. Half of what we thought was zany, cute, clever, or confusing got cut. What remained was a tight, coherent piece about five intersecting lives, with four separate narrative threads and a re-appearing narrator. Could we have gotten there without the long detour through the wilds of our collective imaginings? Perhaps. We have made a few original shows since, and found ways to use time more efficiently. But for our first time out, in retrospect, I think the sidetracks were necessary. None of us could envision the shape of the final piece until we had closed off many pathways of what the piece *was not*. We had to go one way before intuition told us to try something different.

Figure 6.10: Motion Sickness, *Beau Jest Moving Theatre (Elyse Garfinkel, Davis Robinson, and Lisa Tucker), Brimmer Street Theater, Boston, MA, 1989. Photo: Pat Truscello*

As the poet Roethke said in his poem *The Waking*, "I learn by going where I have to go . . . "

Action

As with films, novels, or historical adaptations, have a clear sense of the theme of the piece, especially with original work. Ask yourselves, and make crystal clear, what story are we telling? What truths are we revealing? Why should we care about this piece now? What Risk, Danger, Skill, Joy, Beauty, Fear, Hope, or Pain are we embracing on stage that others may find interesting? What personal needs are being expressed through the theme or topic chosen?

Focus

The most successful original pieces made by Beau Jest were ones that had the clearest focus. *Motion Sickness* worked well because we knew what it was about: the desire to get away from it all. It held up well on tour in different parts of the country with different actors because it had a lot of heart, and the issues dealt with were pretty universal. *The Last Resort* was also a successful piece about a vacation lodge in the Catskill Mountains that couldn't keep up with changing times. This led us to the real theme: letting go of the things we love. The characters came from people the actors actually met at various motels and resorts. We performed in a small theater where live Foley sound effects were easily heard, giving the story a real intimacy that was unique.

Conversely, our holiday show *A Mall and Some Visitors* was a variety show that was fun but too sprawling. *8½* was the result of 8½ weeks of improvisation, a mixture of confessional stories, Frank Capra's *Lost Horizon,* Fred Astaire songs, the Fellini movie, and silly props. The cast was too large (ten) to narrow the show down to one theme, and our time frame was short, so we let it drift and just presented it as a work in progress.

Action

Ask yourselves honestly, is this a piece worth pursuing? Or is it a mess? If you are a professional ensemble and feel that the piece you are working on has no "legs" beyond the opening run, then let it disappear and start your next piece. If it is worth pursuing and if you are a professional group, find more bookings and keep fine-tuning it. If you are a student group, keep the piece alive somehow and make it the first project you produce professionally once you all graduate.

Methods

Beau Jest's most recent project, *Apt. 4D*, was a return to devising an original piece after several years of scripted work. We began with certain limits. We knew it would be created and performed by four actors, with no set or props. We knew the story would involve a lot of movement and playing with light. We knew we wanted the source material to be autobiographical, without being maudlin or self-referential. We knew we wanted to do something a bit dangerous and fun. Because our actors now live in three different states, we had to make do with longer rehearsal days and fewer of them. As I have said elsewhere, some companies do a lot of planning before rehearsals begin. We prefer to brainstorm collectively and focus material as we go along. We picked a theme early on and adjusted it over the year it took us to make the piece. For some really imaginative work, look at what Ping Chong and Company[6] have done with projects inspired by a variety of sources.

Whatever process you use, original plays require a strong motor and a reason to be made. It is impossible to speak in detail about the piece you will make because content dictates form, and your rehearsal process will be different than ours. It must be shaped by the needs of your material. But there are some common patterns to creating original work, so here is 30 years' worth of advice, in short tip format.

Tips

- It's always about something. What "themes" are nagging you these days? Do a few rounds of original monologues with everyone present, and see whether any common patterns emerge.
- Most likely your memories, experiences, relationships, jobs, and current events are going to be the source of many of your ideas in

a piece. It isn't a question of making something from nothing. It's a question of narrowing the possibilities from the zillion ideas you all have to a manageable few.

- Make a stand and say what you want to explore. What is this piece going to be about? What direction is most exciting? Write up a manifesto, or practice saying it to friends. *If you can't say it in a sentence or two, you are probably not sure enough yet of the theme or direction of your work, and the piece will reflect that.*
- Change course as often as you need to, but if you get lost, go back to step three. Keep testing out/describing your work to friends. If they look excited by your enthusiasm and clarity, you are on the right track. If they stare at you dully, you are missing something or haven't yet figured out how to talk about it.
- Find a central image, a location, or an ideograph that unites the piece. Explore all tangents when you come to a fork in the road. If you pose a question with two answers, try both. Choose the more interesting.
- With every new scene or image, more forks in the road will appear. It is like driving down a road with no map. At each fork, pause, try both, and start making lists of all the possibilities you haven't explored yet. Save those lists for when you get lost again later on, and try new scenes out.
- Spend a day going through your old lists "panning for gold". Try all random thoughts and see whether anything new fits. Throw leftovers in the trash.
- Start moving the promising pieces into a sequence; run it and videotape it.
- Watch the tape and determine where there are missing pieces. Write new material, rearrange, and re-tape. Watch.
- Go back to the spine and throw out any bits that detract from it. Test out your new spine by telling friends in a sentence or two what it is about. Dull stares? Do more work.
- Have outside eyes come in and see what you are up to. If you are all in the piece, hire a co-director to watch you from outside. It is really hard to both be in a piece and write it at the same time.
- Make sure your outside eyes are *deep thinkers*. Writing is hard, not everyone can do it, and many very talented performers and designers can't see the forest for the trees. Deep thinkers will frustrate you and infuriate you with casual remarks that may dismiss a whole two months' worth of work, but it is necessary when making something substantial. Deep thinking can be done before rehearsals begin, or during rehearsals, but make sure it happens before the audience comes.

● Get ready to make major changes, and don't get too comfortable with a particular order.
● Check with your fellow actors for personal stories that relate to the theme, and see whether that can influence the piece.

It is very easy to have "nothing" turn into "something" once it has been choreographed and dialogue set. The void now becomes full of moments like "the breakfast scene" and "the travelogue dance". These former bits of nothing now become solid scenes that can move forward or backward as you discover new scenes. These pieces then begin to add up to an outline and, eventually, a show.

Training wheels

Inevitably when you work on an original piece, early scenes that got you to a new level will need to be cut. This is hard. People fall in love with certain moments, or believe they need those scenes to set up the next scene. Transitions you worked on earlier become meaningless because you are going somewhere else now. The whole piece can feel destabilized as you start cutting or moving something that was part of the foundation. Because it is an original piece, there is no way to know whether any of your decisions are the right ones, or whether the choices you are making are heading you into the woods or towards perfection. But the "training wheels" have to come off if intuition or outside eyes tell you a scene is no longer needed. When there is disagreement in the group, some wanting to go left while others want to go right, then clearly there is a problem. You need to solve it, not let it stay status quo. You need to get used to making radical edits and changes up until a few weeks before you open. I find solace in the knowledge that if a change doesn't work you can always go back to what you had. So try bold new choices. You can always fall back on plan A if the new edits don't work (Figure 6.11).

Building the center

Apt. 4D began in part as a reaction to the scale of our previous show, *Ten Blocks on the Camino Real*, whose nine actors, three musicians, and large set were difficult to tour. We knew we wanted to generate a story using autobiographical impulses with four actors that could fit in one car. We used a stylistic prompt – film noir – as a start point. We began by moving together for several weeks, finding phrases that intrigued us. After improvising a range of scenarios and settings, we found a few characters that kept re-surfacing. This led to the image of putting them together on the same floor of a pre-war apartment building, and the story began to gel. The characters became three tenants living on the same floor of a building, intrigued by the arrival of a mysterious new neighbor. The apartment building became the

Figure 6.11: Apt. 4D, *Beau Jest Moving Theatre (Lisa Tucker, Kathleen Lewis, and Robin Smith), Charlestown Working Theater, Boston, MA, 2014. Photo: Davis Robinson*

Figure 6.12: Apt. 4D, *Beau Jest Moving Theatre (Lisa Tucker, Kathleen Lewis, Robin Smith, and Davis Robinson), Charlestown Working Theater, Boston, MA, 2014. Photo: Robert Deveau*

framing device we had been missing, and the show found its center after three months of exploratory work (Figure 6.12).

Unlike *Motion Sickness* and the desire to get away from it all, this piece focused on people who were stuck in their lives and who chose to stay put, attempting to re-invent their lives rather than run away. Every character was at a dead end. One had been fired, one had moved to a new city, and one was an artist who hadn't had a "hit" in 20 years. A new theme developed: the comfort of solitude vs. the need to connect. The noir element became the fourth character, a failed novelist whose want-to-be attempts at writing the next great neo-noir pulp story sucked the other characters on the floor into her ever-escalating fantasies of lurid love, revenge, and murder.

The piece became about finding community, a journey from isolation to connecting with others. Joy was on the roof of the building, and despair was in the basement. Scenes that made no sense to that through-line dropped away. A barometer for when we were talking too much seemed clear to all of us. Dialogue was trimmed to the essential. Outside eyes were brought in to point out new possibilities for scenes and editing. We didn't always have the answers, but we kept working towards a place that seemed more alive, a world we enjoy performing and continuing to explore.

Revisions

After the first performances, we received some excellent feedback from audiences and friends, and encouragement to continue.
We went through a second round of edits and improved some dance and movement sequences during a residency a few months later. There are still some changes we want to make to add danger, surprise, and a few design elements. *Apt. 4D* now feels 90% finished as I write this chapter. Pieces like *Motion Sickness* and *The Last Resort* are in our minds fully mature and dramaturgically complete. *Apt 4D* feels like a show we will continue working on. We plan to tour it for a couple of years. Once we feel it is finished, we will start working on the next project, informed by all that has gone on before us.

Don't worry about whether it is great. Don't worry what the critics will say. Do it for yourselves and your audience. Make the piece you know you have to.

Good luck on your journey, and as the old saying goes, Break a Leg!

7 *Polishing*

This chapter looks at the final phase of the devising process. These principles apply to the final weeks of rehearsal before opening. They can also be used during the run of the show as part of the ongoing process of revision that happens with an ensemble piece if the company is interested in using audience feedback to make further changes.

Feedback

When your work goes public and you get audience feedback, the piece enters a new stage of development. You go back into the studio to make improvements, and fine-tune those parts that aren't working. This is a cycle few actors or designers get to experience in the typical three- to four-week run of a traditional play, as their commitment to the show and each other normally dissolves after a show closes. In the professional theater, a show is considered "locked down" once it opens, and the stage manager is tasked with keeping an eye on the consistency of the production and giving corrective notes to anyone who deviates from the show as directed.

With an ensemble-devised piece, often the dramaturgical work never ends. Companies continue to make changes from night to night and year to year for as long as the piece is performed. Sometimes changes occur when a new actor is brought in to replace someone, or feedback from audiences and critics leads to new ideas. Sometimes the artists want to fix a scene or transition that never felt right, or add something in response to changing times. Some theaters' technical challenges on tour lead to innovative solutions that become permanent changes to all future shows. And sometimes a comment made in passing in the lobby can alert everyone to a problem that was so close to the eyes of the makers that no one had seen the obvious. Polishing and fine-tuning a show before its premiere is a necessity: Continuing that process once it has opened is one of the pleasures of devised work. Some pieces tour for many months, and go through several stages of growth and revision. Some shows can become career defining and last for decades.

An ensemble-devised piece poses several editing and polishing challenges. One is never sure whether the scenes are in the right order; whether a particular song is necessary; whether this should be a movement sequence instead of a monologue; or whether you should do a monologue while dancing at the same time. With Beau Jest, we often polish one song, scene, or dance early in rehearsal because it helps us set the tone for the piece, and gives us a better sense of the theme and direction we are taking. It gives us a shared point of confidence and enthusiasm for the work that helps carry us through the dark times when it feels like the whole piece is a waste of time and we don't know where to turn next (a *very* common feeling on any show). It is at these points that outside eyes are critical, and brainstorming over a beer post-rehearsal may help. After coming up with a rough sequence that we know has good material in it but may still need work, we move into the Editing phase.

Editing

I am always in awe of a well-written, well-executed piece. There is no one path for how a company gets there. If you have a smart writer or director who is watching rehearsals and helping to shape the material, this will save some time. With some shows, we knew early on how the piece began or ended, but spent more time filling in the middle. With others, we struggled with multiple endings until we found the one that fit, but the main story line was clear early on. There is always a balancing act between scenes in a show that you know are effective, and others that are more questionable. Playwrights know that there are scenes they may not like in one of their own plays, but are loath to change it because the weakness in a certain scene may be what gives the next scene its power. To move or change it runs the risk of making the show weaker, not stronger. New shows are often an amalgamation of:

- the original idea that got the ball rolling;
- new material that came out of research during rehearsal;
- new themes pursued when the original idea lost energy or interest in it;
- a synthesis of the new and the original ideas;
- last-minute cuts and changes done for preview audiences.

To determine whether you have all of the right scenes in the right order in any new piece, I generally follow these principles:

- Get the skeleton first before arguing over micro-details.

- Big problems that seem insurmountable can always be broken into smaller, more manageable pieces.
- Stephen Sondheim's dictums, described in his book *Finishing the Hat*, are always useful:
  - *God is in the details.*
  - *Content dictates form.*
  - *Less is more.*
- Videotape rehearsals, review, and discuss frequently.
- Elicit comments from outside eyes. Present them with a rough draft of what you have, and see where they are confused or intrigued.
- Make a list of rocky spots and work on them at the start of every rehearsal. Review material that feels solid. Put your revisions and changes into a new skeleton that is then taped, viewed, and critiqued.
- Go through each character and plot their journey. Do they each have a reason to be in the piece? A goal that is hard to reach, an arc that makes their journey fulfilling or contributes to the bigger story? If you can heighten the stakes, do. If someone serves no real purpose in the story, cut them.
- Make a list of potential new scenes or transitions.
- Spend a couple of days working on new material, test it out and see what sticks.
- Place it into the sequence, tape it again, review and discuss.
- Move material that is working to different places in the show order. Try the ending song as a prelude or interlude, move the opening dance to the middle. See if it improves the flow. Compare to the original sequence and see what feels better, discuss what you gain or lose with each choice. Allow for a day or two of "motion sickness" when making a change, it is always going to feel a little destabilized at first and people will tend to like what is more familiar at first.
- Cut something that isn't working, no matter how long you have spent on it.
- Go back to the spine. What is this piece about? What is needed?
- Try the opposite of what you were thinking. It may open a new door.
- Try the obvious thing you have been resisting doing.
- Keep asking yourselves what world are we in. Does this thing belong? If not, remove it.

You will end up with a trashcan full of discarded scenes, ideas, dances, and material that didn't make it into the final cut and may be fodder for another show. I've never been able to calculate this, but it feels like 80% of what you try ends up in the discard pile.

Final polish

Once Edits are complete, move on to the Polishing phase.
Go through all songs, dances, or skill-based moments to increase the clarity and degree of success with which they are executed. Set all steps precisely, tune up all the singing, bring in specialists to work on accents or combat sequences, clarify transitions, timing, and technical decisions.

   It isn't wise to go on stage until everything has at least a 95% success rate. In other words, if there is a balancing act, a key change, a dance step, a tricky interlocking text sequence, and so on, you should be able to repeat it successfully night after night 95% of the time. Complex technical cues with video, audio, and lighting sequences need to run smoothly. Use the last few rehearsals to go through all places that are "iffy" and make sure everyone is on the right foot, has the words down, knows which direction to turn, knows what their harmonies are. I always save that last 20% of Polishing for when the structural and scripting problems are resolved and we are in the theater with a finished set. It can take hours to do the final fine-tune of one minute of business on stage, and it hurts to cut something after putting that much time into it. Make sure the dance or song is needed before investing days polishing it. I know I am contradicting myself here, but again, it is a balancing act between cleaning things up as you go along so that it is clear enough to see what you have, and getting too involved in polishing the details and minutiae of a moment before you know whether it will be a part of the show. Answer the bigger questions first in broad strokes, then start building in detail, and do your fine-tuning in the last couple weeks of rehearsal.

Outside eyes

It really helps to invite strong critical eyes and thinkers you trust into rehearsal every day, or at a minimum of three different stages. Bring someone in early to bounce ideas off and add to the Big Ideas/frames list; get someone in halfway through to help sort out what is working, what is missing, and make suggestions for new directions; and then make sure your most trusted colleagues and Outside Eyes see the work while final editing is taking place so that they can help you find the flaws before the public does. This is always a delicate time for morale, and you don't want to have to rip apart the entire piece in

the last week of rehearsal, but you do need to hear any hard truths while there is still time to make big changes. This can be actors whose opinion you trust, other directors, or designers, musicians, or choreographers you have worked with or respect.

People in the hallway

I have always found it enlightening to hear unedited, immediate responses to a piece by people who do not know you, do not know what motivated you to make the work, and do not think they are being overheard. This is valuable and sometimes painful feedback, but worth noting. We often think our ideas speak for themselves, but it is good to hear when you are losing people, and what you are losing them over. Or to be pleasantly surprised by what someone saw that you never considered. This does not mean you need to dumb down your work, or remove something challenging. But like politicians who are always surrounded by people who support their views unwaveringly, it is healthy to hear what people "outside the beltway" are saying. It may produce an idea you can work on within the run of a show, or fodder for changes next time you re-mount it. This means eavesdropping on lobby conversation, in the bathrooms, or in the parking lot after a show. If you are a recognizable actor, ask people who had friends there what they heard in the lobby.

Changes in performance

There are artists who script or structure a piece before rehearsals begin, and stick to it right through performance. I can't. We tend to tinker, even when a show is up and running. In a three-week run we might make several small internal changes. With our production of the comic strip *Krazy Kat*, we had several runs over a three-year period that allowed us to make substantial changes between runs. A narrator was cut after the first run and folded into other characters' dialogue. A favorite character, Bum Bill Bee, was cut when we found that as delightful as his moment in the sun was, it was too isolated and unconnected to the rest of the show. A slow dance we all enjoyed made it through two runs before we cut it in run three. Though we were sad to see it go, momentum was better without the dance. When we took *Ten Blocks on the Camino Real* to Provincetown after two short runs in Boston and Maine, we were fairly confident about most of our choices. But Festival director David Kaplan came to see a dress rehearsal and had a flurry of notes that affected tone and rhythm in several places. He knew the play well, and his notes were spot on. One character became a puppet handled by the actress who originally played the part. A powerful switch, made at the last minute.

Fortunately, the actors were confident enough in their roles to be able to absorb his fresh perspectives, and enjoyed rather than resisted the new tempos, challenges, and interpretations.

Time away

Getting some distance is so useful. That can mean taping a rough run-through while you are still in the editing phase, and then putting it on the shelf for a couple of days before looking at it. Take a break from rehearsing. Forget about the show. Then come back to it with fresh eyes and see what you have. Flaws and solutions will be easier to spot. Make a new list to work on.

It can also mean improving a show you have in repertory. If you have created a show and performed it, tape a good run of it with an audience so that you have a record of that version before retiring it. Then when it is booked elsewhere, give yourselves a couple weeks of rehearsal to get back under the hood and make changes while you refresh everyone's memory or incorporate new actors into the piece. Taking a few months off from it before coming back to it will sometimes give you the strength to take on some big changes that are easy to see once you've let it go for a while.

All right, enough talk. Time to get back to the studio. Good luck to you on your devising adventures, and again, Break a Leg! Feel free to call, write, or email me if you have any questions or complaints about this work. It goes without saying that I love devising with others, and do so every summer. If you want to meet in person and do some devising, come to the Celebration Barn for our Devising Intensive, or look at the resources listed in the Appendix for places you can continue training and to find residency programs that invite ensembles to come for a week or two and develop their projects. Best of luck!

Appendix

If you would like hands-on training, here are addresses of some of the major schools currently conducting workshops in devising and ensemble work. There are also new MA and MFA programs with a focus on devising and physical theater in England and the United States that can be find by searching on-line.

Accademia Dell-Arte
PO Box 251505
Little Rock, AR 72225
http://www.dell-arte.org/

The Celebration Barn Theater
RFD 1 Box 236
South Paris, ME 04281
http://www.celebrationbarn.com/

The Center For Movement Theater
Dodi DiSanto, director
PO Box 11655
Washington, DC 20008
301-495-8822
http://www.thisisthecenter.com/cmt.html

The Dell'Arte School
PO Box 816
Blue Lake, CA 95525
707-668-5663
https://www.dellarte.com/

Double Edge Theater
948 Conway Road
Ashfield, MA 01330
http://www.doubleedgetheatre.org/

Ecole Jacques Lecoq
57, Rue du Faubourg Saint- Denis
75010 Paris, France
http://www.ecole-jacqueslecoq.com/en

Ecole Phillipe Gaulier
7 Rue de Bouray
Janville-sur-Juine
91510 France
http://www.ecolephilippegaulier.com/history.html

Frantic Assembly
31 Eyre Street Hill
London, UK, EC1R 5EW
http://www.franticassembly.co.uk/

Margolis Method Center
PO Box 6
Barryville, NY 12719
845-423-2003
http://www.margolismethod.org

NACL Theater
PO Box 33
110 Highland Lake Rd.
Highland Lake, NY
USA 12743
845-557-0694
nacl@nacl.org

The Network of Ensemble Theaters
1709 N. Avenue 56
Los Angeles, CA 90042
323-255-2124
http://www.ensembletheaters.net

Pig Iron Theater
1417 North 2nd Street
Philadelphia, PA 19122
http://pigironschool.org/

Theatre de Complicite
14 Anglers Lane
London, UK, NW5 3DG
http://www.complicite.org/flash/

Notes

1 What Is Ensemble Devising?

1. http://www.beaujest.com/
2. http://www.pigpentheatre.com
3. http://www.maboumines.org/

2 Fundamentals

1. A method of movement analysis developed by F.W. Alexander and used worldwide to reduce tension and improve motor function, alignment, and awareness.
2. https://www.pilobolus.org/home.jsp
3. http://www.mosespendleton.com/
4. http://www.streb.org/
5. http://www.franticassembly.co.uk/
6. http://www.maboumines.org
7. www.celebrationbarn.com
8. http://www.npr.org/2014/10/23/354871509/
herbie-hancock-on-a-path-to-find-my-own-answer
9. http://www.spolin.com/
10. http://www.ecole-jacqueslecoq.com/en
11. http://www.linklatervoice.com/
12. http://www.wakkawakka.org/
13. http://www.nationaltheatrescotland.com
14. http://www.kneehigh.co.uk
15. http://www.improbable.co.uk
16. http://www.margolismethod.org/
17. http://www.amazon.com/To-Actor-Michael-Chekhov/dp/
0415258766
18. https://www.elevator.org/
19. http://www.contactquarterly.com/contact-improvisation/about/cq_
ciAbout.php
20. http://www.bridgmanpacker.org/
21. http://www.tereoconnordance.org/video.php

3 Short Prompts

1. https://www.dellarte.com/
2. http://www.celebrationbarn.com/

3. http://marthaclarke.com/
4. http://www.zaloom.com/
5. http://www.basiltwist.com/
6. http://www.youtube.com/watch?v=JPi56tBDFyM,
7. http://www.youtube.com/watch?v=4NL2QgFs4HM.
8. https://markmorrisdancegroup.org/
9. https://www.pilobolus.org/home.jsp

4   Large Prompts

1. http://www.amazon.com/On-Directing-Harold-Clurman/dp/
   0684826224
2. http://lookingglasstheatre.org/event_types/play-pages/
3. http://mettawee.org/wordpress/
4. http://www.fiascotheater.com
5. http://www.sleepnomore.com/#share
6. http://www.bill-irwin.com/

5   Organizational Structures

1. http://mettawee.org/wordpress/s
2. http://xroads.virginia.edu/~UG01/mincks/brief.html
3. http://cornerstonetheater.org/

6   Full-Length Pieces

1. http://blog.ted.com/2013/07/31/julie-taymor-and-other-creative-
   minds-share-how-they-start-their-incredibly-unique-works/
2. http://en.wikipedia.org/wiki/The_Gold_Dust_Orphans
3. http://www.amazon.com/
   Sense-Direction-Some-Observations-Directing/dp/0896760820
4. http://ripetime.org
5. http://tectonictheaterproject.org
6. http://www.pingchong.org

Recommended Reading

Barker, Clive. *Theater Games.* Portsmouth: Heinemann, 1988

Bogart, Anne. *The Viewpoints Book.* New York: Theater Communications Group, 2004

Britton, John (editor). *Encountering Ensemble.* London: Bloomsbury Methuen Books, 2013

Callery, Dymphna. *Through The Body: A Practical Guide to Physical Theater.* London: Routledge, 2001

Carruthers, Ian and Takahashi, Yasunari. *The Theater of Suzuki Tadashi.* Cambridge: Cambridge University Press, 2004

Crickmay, Chris and Tuffnell, Miranda. *Body Space Image.* University of California: Dance Books, 1993

Govan, Emma, Nicholson, Helen, and Normington, Katie. *Making a Performance: Devising Histories and Contemporary Practices.* London: Routledge, 2007

Graham, Scott and Hoggett, Steven. *The Frantic Assembly Book of Devising Theater.* London: Routledge, 2009

John, Keefe and Simon, Murray (editors). *Physical Theatres: A Critical Reader.* London: Routledge, 2007

Johnstone, Keith. *Impro.* New York: Theater Arts Books, 1979

Kathryn, Syssoyeva and Scott, Proudfit (editors). *A History of Collective Creation.* London: Palgrave, 2013

Lecoq, Jacques. *Le theatre du geste.* Paris: Bordas, 1987

Lecoq, Jacques, Edited by David Bradby. *Theater of Movement and Gesture.* London: Routledge, 2006

Murphy, Vincent. *Page to Stage*: *The Craft of Adaptation.* Ann Arbor: University of Michigan Press, 2013

Nachmanovitch, Stephen. *Free Play.* New York: G.P. Putnam's Sons, 1990

Oddey, Alison. *Devising Theatre – A Practical and Theoretical Handbook.* London: Routledge, 2013

Robinson, Davis. *The Physical Comedy Handbook.* Portsmouth: Heinemann, 1999

Rudlin, John. *Jacques Copeau.* Cambridge: Cambridge University Press, 1986

Rudlin, John. *Commedia dell'Arte: An Actor's Handbook.* London: Routledge, 1994

Simon, Murray and John, Keefe (editors). *Physical Theatres: A Critical Introduction*. London: Routledge, 2007

Spolin, Viola. *Improvisation for the Theater.* Chicago: Northwestern University Press, 1963

Photo credits

Roger Ide, Teresa Izzo, Justin Knight, Bill O'Connell, Davis Robinson, Stanley Rowin, Pat Truscello.

Index

Note: Works by single authors are listed under their names; other plays and productions under their titles.